The Book

Intended for all levels of skill, Margaret Stove's new book, with 236 illustrations and diagrams, is unique in that it is specifically designed to enable knitters to create original hand-knitted lace.

The opening chapter looks back over the years to the sixteenth century and the first knitting to use holes in a decorative manner. Early chapters then discuss the structure of knitting, the 'tools of the trade'—yarns, needles and patterns—and where and when lace can be used to its best advantage.

With accompanying step-by-step pictures and diagrams, the effects of individual stitches are illustrated and explained. Having examined how stitches can be created, readers are invited to participate in specific, carefully described and illustrated exercises. These will extend their skills and, importantly, help make discoveries which will develop and extend their own creative abilities. This is a practical guide.

Having, so to say, 'flexed their needles', readers are then introduced to the important stage of project planning—using tension measurements, charts and construction techniques as a sound base for creating original designs. Instructions are given on how, for future reference, designs can be translated into patterns. Again, each stage is clarified by accompanying diagrams and illustrations. Additionally, the author provides sound advice on how to analyse printed patterns, how to repair damaged lace and how to adapt existing patterns to suit individual requirements.

Having established guidelines, the reader is then provided with a detailed account of how it is possible to progress from the 'visionary' stage of inspiration, through the practical stages of design to the ultimate finished product.

The book concludes with an important set of appendices which include knitting pattern abbreviations. Each has an accompanying descriptive diagram, these are followed by chart symbols (together with a comparison to the major international conventions, including Japanese) and descriptions of construction and finishing techniques.

These useful and essential references are followed by four original knitting patterns designed by the author, a bibliography and an index.

Creating
Original
Hand-knitted

Lace

Creating
Original
Hand-knitted
Lace

Margaret Stove

ROBERT HALE . LONDON

First published in Great Britain
by Robert Hale Ltd, 1995,
Clerkenwell House, Clerkenwell Green,
London ECIR OHT.

ISBN 0-7090-5676-1

Printed in Singapore by Kyodo Printing Co.
(S'pore) Pte Ltd

Contents

Appendices

Acknowledgements

From the time my grandmother taught me to knit, numerous people over many years have contributed to this publication becoming a reality and, although it is not possible for me to mention them individually, it does not mean I do not value and appreciate the rôle they have played.

There are some to whom I owe a special debt of gratitude as they have assisted, encouraged and supported me in more specific ways.

My husband, David, for providing the environment I have needed, especially during the times of 'mental block' and imminent deadlines. For his patience as I have become increasingly occupied by my fascination for this craft and its history—or lack of it. He doesn't even get to wear much of what I now knit as a compensation.

My family, immediate and extended, who over the years have generously shared their knowledge and skills, fostered my interest and as recipients of many of my efforts have tested the product and given me their constructive criticism and advice.

My 'other family', the partners of The Artisan Fibre Centre, with whom I work and whose support and encouragement is of great importance to me. Also to the many members of the New Zealand Spinning, Weaving and Woolcraft Society (NZSWWS) with whom I have been able to share my interest and from whom I have learned so much. In particular I wish to acknowledge the assistance provided in 1986 by the Canterbury area of this organisation which enabled me to extend a visit to Britain to include the Shetland Islands which gave me a first-hand experience of the intricate designs of the Shetland knitters and to cement friendships already formed by correspondence with Gilda Johnson and her mother, Elizabeth, and Mary Jane Peterson.

Jean Abbott, who as NZSWWS National President, recommended me to represent New Zealand at the Arts Festival being held in conjunction with the Commonwealth Games in Edinburgh. This recommendation was endorsed by Edith Ryan, Craft Programme Manager for the Queen Elizabeth II Arts Council of New Zealand until her retirement in December, 1993. I regard this as a major turning point in my attitude to my craft which led to a serious commitment and to my developing the skills I hope I am able to share with readers of this book. For Edith's vote of confidence in my work at this period and for the friendship, time, encouragement and advice she has so generously given me since then, becoming in the process a very dear friend, I thank her most sincerely.

The designs which led to this first major overseas experience may never have 'blossomed' had it not been for early commissions for presentation shawls which gave me the opportunity to experiment with original designs. Thank you Ross and Louise Urquhart for commissioning the first Rata Blossom shawl—later photographed by Stan Jelley—and Allan Innes, representing the High Country Sheepbreeders of the South Island for the commission to design, spin and knit a presentation shawl for the Prince and Princess of Wales to celebrate the birth of Prince William.

Thank you James Mack, then Director of the Dowse Art Museum, Lower Hutt, who 'saw' my designs about this time at a Crafts Council of New Zealand conference. James has continued to challenge, encourage and assist me—especially in the last few years and with Judith MacIntosh Wilson has supported my successful applications for the assistance from the QEII Arts Council which has allowed me to pursue my research into the history and structure of lace in hand-knitting.

Thanks are also due to Elaine Soanes, who as Education Convenor for the 1987 National Woolcrafts Festival at Lincoln College in Canterbury, convinced me to give, for the first time, lectures on my techniques for designing lace. This resulted in my meeting Sue Leighton-White, whose friendly sharing of our common interest I value greatly.

I am particularly grateful to the special people I met overseas such as Mary Walker Phillips, Barbara G. Walker, Hazel Carter, Janet Russell, June Hemmons Hiatt, Catherine Daly, Deborah Robson, Jane Fournier, Frau Blumreich, Dr Helen Bennett, Montse Stanley, Enid Parker, Bishop Richard Rutt, Jeremy Farrell and Dr Charles Casselman. Their generous sharing of their time, knowledge and expertise has added greatly to my own understanding and will, I hope, ensure that a fund of knowledge can grow as more knitters become aware of their work and are able to extend their achievements.

Thank you to all those who have invited me to give seminars and workshops, and especially to those who have participated. Your friendship and willingness to experiment and share knowledge has been so important and is much appreciated.

In turn, I value what I have learned as a student exploring colour and design in classes given by Michael Ebel, Robert McDowell and Michael Reid.

A special thank you to my dedicated knitters, Dorothy Pengelly, Ayleen Coppard and Nancy Reynolds in particular.

This book has been a daunting challenge to my editor, Michael ffolliott-Foster, as he has tried to make sense of the strange language of knitters—especially when there seem to be more exceptions at times than there are rules! Thank you for your patience and perseverance and for not giving up on me. Even the most carefully chosen words can still be clarified and enhanced when accompanied by quality photographs and my thanks go to the official photographer, Edward Field for once again making his skills available and Andrew Johnson who did such an excellent job of photographing 'Mountain Ribbonwood, Arthur's Pass' and the other pieces completed after Edward had left for overseas.

Photographs, for which I am most grateful have also been supplied by Mary Walker Phillips, New York; The Victoria and Albert Museum, London; The Nottingham Costume Museum, Nottingham; The Lerwick Museum, Shetland; Staatliche Kunstsammlungen, Dresden; The Palazzo Pitti, Florence and the Brooklyn Museum, New York.

Thank you to all those at The Caxton Press for being so friendly and helpful. Special thanks to Jack Kempen, Art & Pre-Press Manager and to Graphic Artist, Lisa Ferguson who has transformed and presented my charts and diagrams and prepared the design and artwork so professionally. My thanks, also, to Judith Baker for her most conscientious proof reading.

X

Foreword

Before the 1830s a knitter learnt from her mother or peers. New stitches would be worked into a sampler, which would then serve as a reference tool for future knitting projects. This changed during the 1830s, when the earliest knitting books were published, providing a vast collection of patterns for those who could read and afford to buy the books.

After reading the proof copy of Margaret's book, I went back in time and looked through some of those early knitting books published in the 1830s and 1840s. I could not help but marvel at how hand knitting had developed in the years since then, and why Margaret's book is of such importance in the story of hand knitting.

One of the first to be published was done so anonymously. Later attributed to the Misses Watts, my 1839 3rd edition *The Ladies' Knitting and Netting Book* contains a wealth of fascinating patterns. Of great interest are those associated with knitted lace or in the case of the pattern below, lace knitting:

> *A strong purse. With 2 steel needles and coarse netting silk cast on 60 stitches, knit the first, bring the silk forward, slip a stitch, knit the next, and pull the slipped stitch over the knitted one, bring the silk forward and begin again. The 2nd row is simple knitting.*

No mention of how many rows to complete this strong purse nor how coarse was the netting silk yarn used, these were decisions that the knitters would make. Probably less a problem for the 1830s knitter was the directive to use 2 steel needles. Today we have a wide range of needle sizes from which we could choose, in those days the knitter might have owned only one set of needles and these would be the ones used. Throughout the publication of these early knitting patterns there was a presumption that the knitter knew what she was doing, and did not need to be spoon-fed every little detail.

The explosion of published knitting pattern books in the 1830s continued as a steady flow and was given a further boost by the 1870 Elementary Education Act that eventually meant literacy throughout the nation. *Weldon's Practical Needlework* and *Leach's Practical Fancy Work Basket* magazines commenced publishing in 1886 and led to the inexpensive dissemination of information about needlecrafts.

Somewhere, between there and today, we lost the ability to think in depth about our knitting skills, working by choice from a detailed knitting pattern. Possibly one of the reasons was that from the turn of the century, since the earliest days of pattern publishing by a yarn spinner, the directive was given to use only the yarn spinner's yarns, or the results would not be guaranteed. Knitters felt safer to copy (which is certainly not to be discouraged), but at the same time they lost the ability to develop their own ideas.

Margaret's book will rank as one of the major turning points in the story of the hand knitting of lace. There have been lace knitting books before, her bibliography lists them, but nothing touches the way Margaret has tackled her subject. If a hand knitter follows through from A to Z, they have the chance to emulate the work of their teacher, for Margaret has been most generous in the sharing of her knowledge. And this is the special aspect of her book, the generous sharing and teaching so that any knitter can achieve and aspire to be the hand lace knitter that Margaret has become. They too will be able to draw inspiration for their work from the world around them and know how to convert an idea into a fine piece of lace knitting.

Sue Leighton-White
Western Australia, 1994.

Hand-knitted Laces

ॐ

An Introduction

This book has come into being as a direct result of the numerous requests I have received from members of workshops in the United Kingdom, America, Australia and New Zealand, where we trial-tested many of the techniques which are described in the chapters that follow. Similar requests have also come from colleagues who desire to benefit from the results of workshop testing and who wish to share the material and resources I have collected over the years as I have searched for sources which would show me how to translate my own drawings and thoughts about design.

It is not my intention that this book should document, as might an encyclopaedia, every discovered manipulation of thread and needles. Instead, my purpose has been to present the reader with a range of practical experimentation and discovery which, I very much hope, will stimulate individual creativity and lead to further explorations among the wealth of already published material. I also hope that it will encourage readers to examine closely—and learn from—knitted works in collections and in our everyday environment. For this reason I have included a bibliography, not just to acknowledge the material used in this book, but also to direct the reader towards further opportunities of studying and appreciating additional aspects of this fascinating craft.

The reader should remember that the artistic and creative expression of each individual is unique. Through the pages of this book I have invited you to share my craft-journey with me, however it is important to remember that the way I interpret and use these methods to translate my own ideas may not necessarily reflect the ideas or solutions the reader would choose. This is a guide only and for this reason the patterns given in the appendices at the end of the book are designed to demonstrate techniques and provide take-off points which will enable readers to move off in directions of their own choice.

It is to be hoped that this book will also inspire knitters to use printed patterns, not just as a recipe for a particular article but, importantly, as an exercise in understanding more about

1

the structure of knitting—why the pattern works—and then to take a step forward and explore variations.

The patterns in the appendices are presented in both written and chart form so as to provide a further means of enabling the reader to consolidate an understanding of how one version relates to the other.

Selecting appropriate exercises in order to establish a foundation which makes it possible for a knitter to embark on original work has proved to be a considerable challenge. There have been occasions when I have experimented with ideas, usually in a workshop situation, only to discover that an assumption I have made has proved to have been impractical. At such times the input of my craft classes has been invaluable and underlines the importance of putting ideas to the test before progressing with theoretical assumptions.

Learning from a book presents several challenges and is more likely to be successfully accomplished if the sequence of steps set out by the author is consistently followed and if suggestions about possible extensions to a basic principle are fully explored. For most of us this needs considerable motivation and a measure of self discipline. A workshop environment may be an excellent stimulus and means of achieving intentions; however a book has the advantage of always being there to refer to, so providing the reader with time for considered experimentation.

For those who are already familiar with charts, it will be obvious that most of the charts could be condensed by not including each repeat. For those learning this technique for the first time, however, it is helpful to have a visual representation of the actual knitting so that it becomes possible to isolate any problems which may occur. This also explains why the chart for the 'Flowering Eucalyptus' border has been given in an expanded form.

In my search for ways to describe more easily my approach to self-designed, hand-knitted lace, I have learned so much more about techniques and approaches that I can hardly wait to begin work on the new ideas and alternatives that have presented themselves. Since becoming involved and exploring creative possibilities, I have discovered wonderful books and pieces of knitting, but the greatest bonus of all has been the opportunity to meet and work with so many talented and dedicated knitters.

It is my sincere hope that readers may be able to find techniques in this book which will lead them to discovering the joy of unique creations.

1. Historical Background

❧

Lace in Hand Knitting—When did it begin?

Assembling this book has been somewhat akin to embarking on the construction of a jigsaw puzzle with a large part of the picture missing and no guarantee that all the pieces will be there. However, there are enough pieces to tantalize and also to create a strong desire to see the completed picture, even if some parts must be left to the imagination and, by getting started who knows when and from where more of the pieces may turn up?

The information contained in this book has resulted not only from personal experience, but also from what I have discovered in my search for information which will provide answers to the many questions that have arisen for me as I have explored ways, with a particular focus on lace, of translating my own designs and ideas into knitted fabric.

Over recent years there has been an upsurge of interest in making unique, knitted garments and decorative pieces and this has resulted in the development and use of colour, texture and designer yarns. The latter exploring not only the use of traditional natural fibres but also of synthetics and non-traditional materials. It has been an exciting adventure discovering how knitters and spinners of the twentieth century, using their respective skills along with this diversity of materials—whether natural or synthetic, produced by hand or machine — have found such progressive forms of expression and have as a result created a new popularity for this time-honoured craft.

Sometimes lace is included either as a highlight in an over-all design or, quite often it plays a major role in these creations. Generally, lace in such designs is mainly devised by using existing patterns in innovative ways and extending them with variations. Up to this time, with some notable exceptions, I have found very little of an in depth nature to assist the aspiring designer of original openwork patterns. The exceptions being, *Creative Knitting* by Mary Walker Phillips, in which the author shares the techniques she employs and the variety of unusual materials

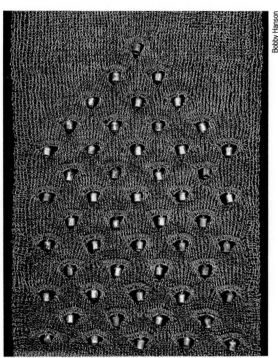

Bobby Hanson

Figure 1.
Mary Walker Phillips, Knitted
Metal and Indian Bells, 'Bells
for Dunedin 1981', private
collection—Catherine Daly.

she uses for creating her unique pieces as illustrated in Figure 1; *The Batsford Book of Hand and Machine Knitted Laces* by Tessa Lorant; *Charted Knitting Designs* by Barbara Walker and, more recently, *Knitting Lace* by Susanna Lewis. Even these exceptions, beyond illustrating useful techniques with suggestions and examples of how they may be used, do not provide practical exercises to facilitate a beginner's progress in original design. Consequently, I have needed to resort to my own experience, observation and experimentation, with constant recourse to the already mentioned authors, together with Mary Thomas, Marianne Kinzel, Elizabeth Zimmerman, Barbara Abbey, Annette Feldman and, more recently June Hemmons Hiatt, as well as the *Mon Tricot* and *Burda* publications, to increase my range of skills in the use of techniques and to devise ways of isolating, or combining these, sometimes in conjunction with my own variations, to produce the effects I am striving for.

It is hard to be specific as to when my particular 'adventure' began, as the fund of knowledge from which I have drawn has been built up over many years and would be typical of the way most of us build up the skills we require for particular interests.

For as long as I can remember, knitting has been part of my family. My maternal grandparents lived with us for most of my early childhood and after much pestering, my 'nana', who was invariably knitting when she wasn't in the garden, relented and taught me to knit when I was four years old. I was to discover much later that my grandmother's Danish background resulted in my being taught the continental method of knitting. This speedy method has been a tremendous advantage and has added to the attraction of pursuing this rather labour-intensive craft. The main difference with this method is that the yarn is held in the left hand, close to where the new stitch is being made, thus saving unnecessary movement.

Like most small children my first efforts were laboured and fraught with all the problems of dropped stitches, unplanned increases and variable tension. However, there is little to compare with the elation at such a young age of seeing 'real fabric' emerging and, with further practice, eventually to be in control of the end product.

It was on Victory Day in 1945, when I was five years old, that I passed my grandmother's test of efficiency in stocking stitch and was taught how to knit rib. I can still recall vividly, her telling me to knit the 'V's for victory and to purl the crosses, the latter being formed by the loop of the purled stitches. But for some reason the real Red Letter Day for me was learning to knit my first lace pattern. This was 'Feather and Fan' as my grandmother always called it, or 'Old Shale', according to the Shetland tradition. She wrote this down for me as I was now at school and well into learning to read, and I will never forget my delight at being initiated into the meaning of knitting pattern abbreviations. It may be interesting to note that the patterns which she used at this time employed the abbreviations 'm1' or 'wfwd' to describe placing the yarn over the needle to make a new stitch. This early introduction to the term 'make 1' used as a 'yarn over' has later led me both to cause and experience much confusion.

However, during this period I ran into other difficulties as I tried to interpret patterns for myself from knitting books and magazines. What a patient lady she was when she rescued me from confusion as I tried to understand and carry out such instructions as 'rep. from * to * to end.' Needless to say it was from making mistakes that I began to discover some interesting facts about how patterns are constructed and from time to time abandoned the pattern book in order to explore an accidental variation. For this reason I am a firm believer in one of my family's favourite sayings—'that a mistake is only a mistake if you don't learn something from it.'

As with any medium, proficiency and pleasure come from personal practice and experimentation and this early 'playing' with stitches allowed me, quite unconsciously, to build up a wonderful resource to draw upon later when I came to design my own patterns.

Learning to knit is to become part of an association of people which is world wide and goes back into the mists of antiquity. It is a fascinating history to explore and there are many publications available today for those who are interested in reading about the development of this craft. The most notable, recent publication being *A History of Hand Knitting* by Richard Rutt. His bibliography provides a wealth of material for those who wish to obtain an even deeper knowledge of this fascinating subject than that given in his text.

I felt it would be most appropriate, before embarking on the subject of my book, to look first at the origins of this particular form of the craft as a starting off point, and to revise and consolidate my knowledge of the structure of lace in hand knitting. I imagined this as being a relatively simple and attractive task requiring several enjoyable hours of reading and taking notes. The exercise has led to a far more extensive period of research than I could ever have imagined, and my results to date still leave many questions unanswered.

The difficulty I have experienced in finding specific details describing the beginnings of lace in knitting, which for this purpose I will define as the use of open work, eyelets or holes in a purely decorative sense, has led me to believe that because of this function, its practice has probably occurred comparatively recently, which would explain why there is little mention or evidence of lace in knitting before the sixteenth century.

There is ample evidence of bobbin laces from a much earlier period and the subjects of many portraits wear accessories elaborately adorned with such laces. These laces are used with fine woven fabrics, often in conjunction with rich embroideries.

With the assistance of the Queen Elizabeth II Arts Council of New Zealand, I have been able to explore this particular form of knitting a little further, not only the history but also its structure, which brings up questions, such as what is *lace knitting*? and is *lace knitting* different from *knitted lace*? After much reading and discussion with several mentors it appears that it is generally accepted that lace knitting is defined as a knitted fabric where there is a row of plain knitting worked alternately with a row of holes made in various ways. Whereas *knitted lace* is a knitted fabric where the holes are made on every row.

The easiest way to identify into which category a piece of lace falls, is to look at the yarn which separates holes lying above one another. The lace knitting has twisted strands of yarn and the knitted lace has a single strand of yarn making the separation. This makes the appearance of the latter to be more like 'true lace' which is woven with bobbins. These constructions are shown in Figures 2 and 3. However, there can be exceptions and careful note of the results of knitting the chart in Figure 43 given for sample 2b in Chapter 3 is an example.

There are also laces which are knitted which do not fall exactly into either of the first two categories, and for which

Figure 2. Example of knitted lace.

Figure 3. Example of lace knitting.

7

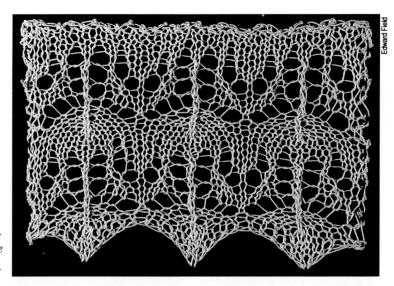

Edward Field

Figure 4. 'Lotus Flower' pattern. A combination of knitted lace and lace knitting.

there is no official description, as using unorthodox methods is often the best way to achieve a desired result. Figure 4.

It appears that the first knitting to use holes in a decorative way would have been on hosiery made in the sixteenth century. This was about the time when knitted fabric was replacing cloth for such items as gloves and sleeves, as well as hose, and no doubt included other items of underwear. Many of these garments were knitted from silk and there are references to silk stockings worn by Elizabeth I and a preference for these over cloth stockings. As bobbin lace would not have had the elasticity required to complement knitted fabric, and as such stockings would have been worn by the rich who, as portrayed in paintings of that period, wore clothing richly decorated with laces and embroideries, one could easily conclude that a need would have arisen to create a similar lace effect with knitting.

Figure 5 shows a photograph of a miniature painted by Nicholas Hilliard. The subject is Sir Christopher Hatton (1540—1591). It was painted at the time he was appointed Lord Chancellor in 1587 and he is shown wearing white stockings with an elaborate all-over diamond eyelet pattern. The extraordinary attention to detail in the painting actually includes the shaping for the heel and instep of the stocking. For a painting of such small dimensions (56 x 43 mm) such accuracy is invaluable in establishing milestones in the story of lace that is knitted.

Figure 5. Elaborately patterned knitted stockings of Sir Christopher Hatton. Reproduced by courtesy of the Victoria & Albert Museum, London.

In *Legacy of Lace* by Kathleen Warnick and Shirley Nilsson, it is recorded that Mary Queen of Scots in 1575 sent Queen Elizabeth head-dresses, collars, cuffs and nightcaps she had knitted. This is one of many similar references for which there does not seem to be any proof but they do indicate that during this period such items were available and, if not locally made, were being imported into England.

In Europe, a pair of silk stockings which were probably originally crimson, were found in 1857 in the tomb of Eleanora of Toledo, wife of Cosimo I de' Medici, Grand Duke of Tuscany, who died of malaria in 1562. These stockings have a turn over top which features arrangements of four eyelets contained in diamond shapes of reverse stocking stitch. This example, although very simple, appears to be the earliest pair of stockings for which an accurate date is available. Figure 6.

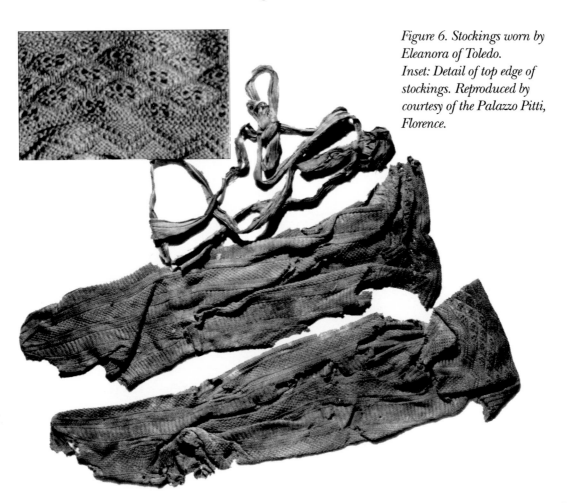

Figure 6. Stockings worn by Eleanora of Toledo.
Inset: Detail of top edge of stockings. Reproduced by courtesy of the Palazzo Pitti, Florence.

Probably the earliest example of the decorative use of openwork which has a reliable date, are the knitted silk breeches which have been featured in several publications. These are shown in Figure 7. The silk is yellow and the breeches are lined with yellow taffeta and natural-colour goat leather. They are at present in the collection of the Dresden Museum and are dated between 1552-1555. They belonged to August (b.1526), the Elector of Saxony (1553-1586) and are listed in his 1555/1556 dress-inventory. The alternate panels of sloped faggot stitch forming arrowheads are divided by slits as they have been knitted separately and then, when all the panels have been completed, the knitting is continued across all stitches thus joining them into one piece. The breeches also demonstrate successful solutions to complex problems of shaping which would have required a sophisticated knowledge of the structure of knitted fabric.

I was disappointed that so many of the books I consulted on early costume and dress of various countries had very little to say about undergarments, hose and other accessories, when there are such strong indications that the first use of lace in

Figure 7. Yellow, silk breeches which belonged to August, elector from Saxony. Inset: Detail of design. Reproduced by courtesy of Staatliche Kuntsammlungen, Dresden.

knitting would have been to embellish garments such as these. However, from the few examples available it does appear that these early designs were arrangements of simple eyelets and vertical and diagonal faggot stitch similar to those in the above illustrations.

During my visit to the Costume Museum in Nottingham, England, I was delighted to discover a pristine example of fine, knitted silk gloves which had a simple lace zigzag pattern and were also edged with a bobbin lace. Figure 8. They are described as 'a man's gloves dated 1600—1650'. This museum has several excellent examples of well preserved very early knitting, as well as interesting pieces of more recent lace that is knitted.

Figure 8. Man's silk gloves 1600-50. Reproduced by courtesy of the Museum of Costume & Textiles, Nottingham.

Included in a fascinating article, 'The Knitting Crafts of Europe from the Thirteenth to the Eighteenth Century', by Dr. Irena Turnau on page 20 in Volume 65, 1982, Numbers 1 & 2 of *The Bulletin of the Needle and Bobbin Club* are several reproductions of Spanish, French, Italian, German and West Pomeranian knitters, as well as knitting factories and various examples of guild trademarks. It is interesting to note that these all seem to feature stockings, indicating again that these were commonly knitted garments.

Even more frustrating has been the allusion to legends, such as that recorded by Kathleen Warnick and Shirley Nilsson in

Legacy of Lace, that Saint Brigid, who died in 1335, introduced lace knitting to Sweden. It is purported that, at the age of twelve, she was guided in this art by her guardian angel!

There is often confusion caused by the difficulty in identifying with certainty some of the methods used in early times to produce 'knitted fabric'. It is also frustrating that statements, such as those included in James Norbury's *Traditional Knitting Patterns*—and later repeated in more recent knitting books claiming that the origin of lace knitting as being Spanish—cannot be authenticated with documented evidence. However, Spain, France and Italy have certainly provided a treasure trove of lace of both great beauty and variety from a period when lace knitting could have been regarded as a natural development of knitting skills which were well established in Europe.

The availability of suitable fine yarns for knitting lace has also been significant to the establishment of this style of knitting and accounts for its popularity in early nineteenth-century England and Scotland when fine Merino wool was available from the continent, as well as silk and fine cottons. It is during this period that the lace of Shetland, spun and knitted from the local sheep, became established and different areas of the country specialized in different articles, with Unst and Lerwick famous for producing the remarkable 'wedding ring' shawls. Figure 9.

Figure 9. Fine Shetland shawl, knitted by a member of the Priest family in 1918. Reproduced by courtesy of the Lerwick Museum, Shetland.

However, I have discovered another tradition about superfine ring shawls of lace knitting which, according to Galina Khmelera, St Petersburg, Russia, and Ingrid Bengis, Maine, United States of America, goes back at least three hundred years. They showed me modern examples of exquisite hand-knitted shawls, using the finest cashmere, handspun on supported spindles and plyed with fine, commercially spun silk. Originally the latter would have been handspun also. The needle size used is quite large in relation to the grist size or thickness of the yarn, but most of the shawls would easily pull through a 'wedding ring'. They are made by families in the village of Orenburg, to the South of the Ural mountains and situated on the old silk route. The cashmere is combed from the animals and the children remove the guard hairs; at present there are approximately two hundred people involved in producing such shawls. The patterns used are quite distinctive, as shown in Figure 10, and are similar to a Russian shawl (catalogue number T17898), possibly of blended cashmere and wool and dated at around 1869, which is in the storage area of the Smithsonian National Museum of American History, Washington DC, United States of America. This example has a fringed edge which was a usual method of finishing these shawls at that time, however the more recent examples have a zigzag knitted edging.

I have also read a translation by Jan Butler of *The Pure Spring— Craft and Craftsmen of the USSR* by Alexander Milovsky,

Edward Field

Figure 10. Orenburg Stole
Inset: Detail of corner edging.

Raduga Publishers, Moscow, where the fibre of the goats is described in detail and it is claimed that the Orenburg breed is unique and, in spite of attempts to establish them in England, France and the New World as early as 1818, this did not prove to be successful. The quality of the fibre is said to be rivalled only by the wild Tibetan Kashmir goat which is a related strain and there are those who claim the Orenburg product to be superior.

There is little doubt that the recording and handing on of the earliest patterns was by word of mouth and in the form of samplers, as most of those practising the craft to make what we would regard to be a very frugal living, would have been illiterate. The recent publication of *Knitting Lace* by Susanna E. Lewis is based on a sampler which is in the Brooklyn Museum in the United States of America. Figure 11. It is thought to have been made in southern Germany or Austria in the early to the mid-nineteenth century. It is worked in a natural colour, 3-ply cotton

Figure 11. Sampler.
Reproduced by courtesy of the
Brooklyn Museum, New York.

thread and measures 457cm (15ft) and is made up of 91 patterns with 45 to 50 stitches in each pattern, including selvages. The average width is 9cm (3.5ins). It was not until knitting books began to appear, from about 1835, that knitting became a popular and fashionable, leisure pursuit. The earliest recorded printed publication, in 1836 in Britain, was the first of many by Jane Gaugain and one such is said to have included a pattern for an elaborate lace stocking copied from a Maltese original. Mrs Gaugain also invented her own abbreviations, however other writers did not follow suit and a completely different set were invented in 1906 for *Weldon's Practical Needlework*. Right up to the present day there are differences, as can be seen in Appendix A, in the meanings of knitting terms and abbreviations used.

A major surprise for me was to discover that knitting appears to have been introduced into Japan much earlier than I had expected, with the earliest possible date being during the Namban era (1567 to 1635) as, according to Nobumasa Sakata and Michael Harvey in an article '400 Years of Knitting in Japan', the 'Namban' used in naming the era refers to Spain and Portugal, from whence ships had traded since the middle of the Heian era (10th century A.D.) and it appears as though the first garments traded were, once again, stockings! It is also claimed that 'Meriyasu', which is what the Japanese call knitting, originated from the Spanish word for stocking, which is 'medias'. Today, in spite of so much Japanese home knitting being done on knitting machines, there are many books available which have charts and translations of numerous European, lace patterns, in particular, the lace patterns of Herbert Neibling, which were originally published by *Burda*. In Appendix A I have included one version of symbols used in a modern, Japanese lace knitting book.

It is interesting to note the various forms in which versions of lace are knitted. There are three very different styles worth mentioning which are not seen very often and are worthy of further study. One of these is very obviously based on a style of bobbin lace, in that a free-form design of solid area, varying sized holes and a raised outline are worked on a mesh background of faggots. The only examples I have seen have been a photograph in Figure 94 in *Mary Thomas's Knitting Patterns* which has the caption 'Knitted Laces', eighteenth to nineteenth century. Freehand design', and in a Danish publication belonging to Montse Stanley who operates a 'knitters' reference facility' from Cambridge in England, there are, among other things, an illustration depicting small portions of three edgings using this same technique. Until now I have not been able to learn anything more of this technique.

The other two methods resemble forms of crochet and are also described, along with variations in, *Mary Thomas's Knitting Patterns*. Betty Franks, who writes a series entitled 'Dentelles' for the Australian magazine, *Textile Fibre Forum*, also describes both these methods in volume 37, 1993.

The first which she refers to as 'Picot Point Knitting', looks just like an imitation of Irish Crochet. It is made by casting on small numbers of stitches and then casting them off, building up a length of picots and then joining them in various ways. Larger motifs, like flowers and leaves, are knitted as free-form pieces and are also incorporated in the mesh formed by the joined picots. A friend from Kent, England, has recently sent me a copy of a small booklet with a variety of projects using this method, but unfortunately there is no publisher's name or date of publication.

Those readers familiar with Filet Lace crochet will recognise the second method, which is a knitted version of the square mesh of open and solid blocks which is the basis for this form of lace. I have used this at times for my own designs and an example of this is the insertion for Prince William's shawl shown in Figure 86, Chapter 5.

From my thorough search through all the materials which, at this stage, have been available to me, it does not seem possible to be specific about a time or place where the first appearance of knitted lace predates the already mentioned breeches and stockings. This opens up a challenge to those interested, to continue the search and perhaps discover a clearer picture of what prompted the creation of not only the elaborate, highly decorative laces, but also the more simple favourites of many generations which continue to give so much pleasure to knitters today.

2. The Structure of Knitting

ଚ∿

Definitions, materials and equipment

Before embarking on a study of how to use hand-knitting to design original lace it is necessary to consider the structure of hand-knitted fabric and how to define the manipulations required to achieve the results envisaged. One of the facts which became increasingly obvious when researching the history of this form of knitting was that both the words 'knitting' and 'lace' have origins which, like many words in the English language, have several meanings and uses. For example we use the word 'knit' to mean fuse when we refer to bones healing, also to indicate unity and from earlier times methods of holding materials together. There are even fabrics which, on first sight appear to be knitted as we would define knitted fabric today but which are made using techniques which are quite different and have very ancient beginnings, see Figures 12, 13, & 14.

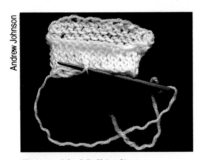

Figure 12. Nalbinding.

Figure 13. Tunisian crochet.

Figure 14. Tablet weaving bag made by Daphne Erasmus.

In Richard Rutt's Introduction to his book, *A History of Knitting*, he refers to the phrase 'knitting cup' as used in Ben Jonson's play *The Magnetic Lady* written in 1632, where 'knitting' means 'marriage'. In some languages the same word is used for both knitting and crochet, in spite of the structure and the equipment to produce such end products being quite different.

However, for the purpose of this study knitting will be classed as a structure where a continuous thread makes four changes of direction and is accomplished with two needles, even though there may be more than two needles holding a supply of stitches. Figure 15.

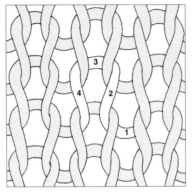

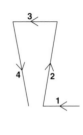

Figure 15. Structure of Knitting.

The direction of the individual stitches and their position within the fabric are arranged by the knitter to create particular effects.

Similarly, although as knitters we are more inclined to think of lace in its noun form, as a design of decorative holes its original, verbal meaning is 'to snare' and the noun to mean the cords or thongs which are used to snare. For example, we lace our shoes. As our ancestors used nets and similar devices to catch and ensnare, the later use of a net as a background for further embellishment provides a good link for describing this art as lace.

Having discovered that traditionally, lace in knitting falls into two categories, *knitted lace* and *lace knitting*, there is still the problem of what to call lace which is knitted but does not fall strictly into either of these categories. How do we refer to those designs which can be made up of a mixture of the traditional forms and can also incorporate a manipulation of stitches which give the effect of lace but, although an openwork effect or hole is created, this is not necessarily obtained by the placing of the yarn over the needle? After discussing this question with several knitters who have a special interest in this subject, it was decided that probably *creative lace*, as favoured by Mary Walker Phillips, is the best term to use.

Other definitions which need to be considered are terms such as design and pattern, especially as the latter term is generally used by knitters in the sense of a formula or set of instructions. It will be less confusing if this definition continues to be used in this way and to describe the plan or arrangement of the elements being used to express an idea as the design.

Lace in knitting, unlike other knitted fabrics, has an extra dimension which needs to be considered when it is used for a design, whether or not it is for apparel or for a purely decorative piece. As it is constructed from solid and open areas through which a background can be seen, all three components of solid, open and background areas must be taken into account, as they all play a role in the total appearance of the article. For this reason it is necessary to design with this in mind. In fact, this aspect can be used to great advantage to enhance not only the most intricate of designs, but also relatively simple patterns.

At this point it may be timely to share the best piece of advice I have ever received in relation to design. It was given at a seminar I attended on Design for Craft given by Colleen O'Connor, an art teacher of many years experience. It was given as 'The Artist's Prayer' and was as follows:

'Simplify, simplify, simplify. Amen'

Very easy to learn, very easy to remember but not always so easy to carry out!

I urge all lace knitters to make it their own, as it is very easy to get carried away with patterns because their finished appearance give the impression of one's mastery of a difficult discipline. However, even more satisfying is the use of these technical skills—combined with good design skills—to achieve a truly memorable result which is the unique personal expression of the craft artist.

Another important consideration, which can often be overlooked, is the time involved, the cost of materials and the possible life of the article in relation to the value—sentimental or otherwise—of the finished product. These are decisions which, in the end, only the craftsperson can make, but which must be evaluated before undertaking a project—especially major undertakings. I wonder how many of us qualify for the fellowship of those who have unfinished projects abandoned and lying in the backs of cupboards, mainly because they were embarked upon without proper thought about the time available, our capabilities or our expectations of the result.

I am not suggesting that it is not good to be a little over-ambitious at times, or to try something completely different. All these experiences teach and extend us.

In fact, a good approach to this craft is a sense of adventure and a realisation that 'mistakes' are often the beginning of a whole new range of exciting discoveries just waiting to be explored in full. However, there are occasions when it can also become very discouraging and even expensive; when a little forethought could have resulted in the warm glow of a new accomplishment and a subsequent motivation to seek for even greater achievements.

It is now time to look at some of the special criteria that need to be considered when designing projects using lace fabric.

Apparel

Designing a garment is a really challenging exercise for the lace knitter. As well as aiming to achieve an overall pleasing effect, the age of the wearer and the purpose of the garment must all be taken into account.

Of primary consideration is the suitability of using a lace fabric for the planned item. For obvious reasons there are times when lace is quite unsuitable, for example, a jersey for a fisherman! Sometimes it is not so obvious and the materials used could also play a major role in making an appropriate decision.

From my experience it appears that baby garments are among the most popular items for those wishing to try their hand at knitting lace. This is probably because the garments are small and seem less daunting than large projects and the news of a new arrival can provide strong motivation to make something special. So the following points will illustrate the kind of considerations which must be taken into account when planning for a specific use.

1) Choice of materials must be the first concern, especially if the garment is to be worn next to the skin. Importantly, the age of the baby will also influence this choice, as a newborn baby's skin is far more delicate than that of an older baby or toddler. It should also be noted that natural fibres, in particular wool and cotton, are more appropriate for babies.

Yarns with loose or a potential for loose fibre must be avoided for very young babies as they can cause irritation and may be inhaled.

2) Simplicity of garment shape, to allow for easy dressing and comfort.

3) Placement of lace patterns with large areas of openwork need to be where they will not allow tiny fingers and toes to be caught.

4) Fastenings, whether buttons, domes (US press-studs) or ties, should be located where they are safe and will not cause discomfort.

5) The grist of the yarn and choice of needle gauge to produce an appropriate fabric for the garment.

6) Placement of the motifs should be in harmony with the overall design of the garment.

An example of (3), in relation to the design of a baby shawl, would be ensuring that the areas most likely to come into contact with fingers and toes are of denser fabric and more intricate openwork than that used to embellish the borders. Extra-special shawls, for Christenings and so on, can be of a more elaborate overall design if a fine, plain fabric wrap is used as a liner.

Heels, toes and elbows of garments also need to be of a denser fabric, in order to be comfortable, safe and durable.

For (6) an example would be deciding where the attention should be focused to enjoy the design. During the first few months of a baby's life, when the baby is often held against the shoulder, the back of the garment is an ideal area for an elaborate pattern. The sleeves and lower border of the garment, with a special emphasis on the area from the knees down on a long gown, are also excellent pattern areas. Small fussy areas around the front of the bodice are rarely seen and are subject to damage and so are better left plain. Lace in knitting for older children and adults is more likely to be in the form of accessories, trimmings or lightweight vests, jerseys (US sweaters) and less likely for larger items.

Similar criteria as discussed above apply to designing articles incorporating or made entirely of lace for older children and adults. There is obviously much more potential to use a variety of fibres and, with the garments being so much larger, there is plenty of scope for organising really interesting lacy areas to be displayed to the best advantage. However, remember that the

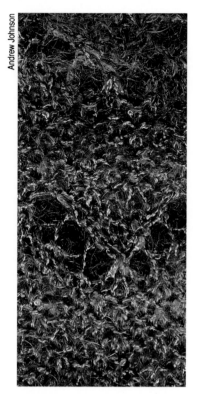

Andrew Johnson

Figure 16. Detail of mohair and rayon waistcoat.

final product must be comfortable and work for the purpose for which it is intended.

Today we have a wide range of new yarns to work with and even the traditional fibres of wool, cotton, silk and linen have been given new rôles. As well as a variety of spinning techniques and finishes which often improve their durability, they are available in exciting blends, textures and colour effects. Each season brings new concepts in yarn design from the manufacturers and fashion houses. These provide the creative knitter with a wealth of inspiration and a never ending resource for experimentation. One of my favourite projects was knitting a waistcoat from a space-dyed skein of yarn which was spun entirely from synthetic fibre. A fluffy, mohair type viscose was plyed with a very shiny rayon thread. The colours having a really jewel-like effect on the rayon. The waistcoat was knitted on size 4.5mm needles (UK & US 7) to make space for the 'fluff'. Bands of moss stitch and a very simple zigzag lace pattern were used, with the decreases in the latter making a surface chain effect, allowing the rayon to outline the lines of holes and accentuate the purl stitches of the moss stitch. (Figure 16)

Ultimately, when something special like a wedding gown is your chosen project, then good planning and sampling are essential to ensure a successful result and thus avoid disappointment and unnecessary expense. Having first-hand experience of such a project, I also came to realise very quickly that, when deciding on the grist of yarn and needle gauge, this is one of the occasions when the amount of time involved for the total project must be taken into consideration. Whereas a shawl may be used on many occasions, including adult fashionwear as well as for a baby, a wedding gown is unlikely to be used for more than the one occasion or, at the most, once each generation. Consequently, if the desired effect can be achieved using a larger needle size and thicker yarn than for a Christening shawl, then it makes good sense to do so.

Lace in knitting does not need to be restricted to apparel, as any study of lace knitting books, old and new, will reveal. There are many beautiful patterns for curtains, coverlets and other decorative pieces and these can provide some very interesting challenges, as well as providing the opportunity of exploring a wide variety of materials. Mary Walker Phillips in her book, *Creative Knitting : A New Art Form*, ably demonstrates how the seemingly most unlikely materials can be used to create impressive decorative articles rather than solely functional items.

Her work involves the use of such materials as leather, fibreglass and even copper wire!

There are many instances where lace that is knitted is being used in new and exciting ways. In Jan Messant's knitting books, particularly *Wool 'n Magic*, there are many and varied examples of the imaginative use of lace that is knitted often being incorporated into pieces using crochet and embroidery as well. There are many other artists exploring the use of knitting as a medium for original design and I hope that the exercises, observations and projects that follow will be of assistance to those who wish specifically to use lace to express their ideas and that this will lead to more discoveries which will be enjoyed and shared.

I do not intend to repeat the comprehensive material which can already be found in many published books on the principles of knitting and in collections of knitting patterns, but I will include a bibliography for those who wish to have access to this material. It is rather my intention to draw on these resources to provide examples of how they may be used to devise original articles using lace and then explore ways of translating original designs for lace into knitting.

For most of us this latter step is the peak of our ambition and there are no easy ways of solving all the problems along the way; however, I have discovered there are methods which can provide assistance, and with perseverance, the breakthroughs generally come and are especially rewarding.

As lace projects can cover such a wide range there are several categories which can be considered separately when deciding on appropriate equipment and materials.

Enthusiasm in making decisions about the appropriate yarn and needle size for our chosen design can result in overlooking the fact that we often have a choice of equipment as well, and that the correct choice can be of considerable importance to the enjoyment of our craft both now and in the future!

One thing I have learned after so many years of constant knitting, and from discussion with other knitters, is that as well as considerable pain and discomfort occurring when one knits for prolonged periods, there is also a very real danger of permanent injury. Unfortunately, many of us find out when the damage is done. When my children were at home I used to long for the day when I could knit without constant interruptions. My wish was eventually granted, only to discover that those interruptions were ensuring that the muscles involved in my craft were being rested and my posture regularly changed.

Knitting any pattern which requires concentration, resulting in protruded neck posture for long periods, causes overstretching of ligaments and eventually distortion of the discs contained in the vertebral joints.

Danger signals to be aware of are pain at the base of the neck, headaches spreading from this area, a burning sensation across the shoulders, pain in the elbows and/or wrists and tingling in the fingers. There are many helpful exercises which can be most beneficial, however it is much better to avoid the problem altogether by practising good posture and changing position regularly. I try now to organize my day's work to include wherever possible suitable activities which alternate with periods of knitting.

The choice of equipment to be used can also help lessen stress on muscles and I now use, if the choice is available, needles which are flexible. When I discussed this injury problem with Shetland knitters it was interesting to discover that to them it did not seem to be of any real concern. Maybe wearing the knitting belt shown in Figure 17, which supports the long double pointed needles which they use, helps to minimise the stress on the muscles involved in knitting. Some people find that using circular needles, especially with projects which are heavy, is also helpful. A cushion strategically placed under the arm or elbow can also assist, but the best solution of all is regularly to return the head to its rightful position, directly over the vertebral column and allow the arms to relax from the shoulder.

Choosing materials for the very finest laces would be from a similar range to those used for 'true lace' projects, such as edgings, doilies, accessories and decorative pieces which look well in fine cotton, linen and silk; with the choice of knitting needles being in the range of 2mm and finer. Unfortunately, the needles available in this size range are generally limited to

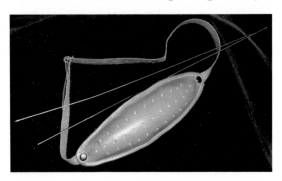

Figure 17. Knitting belt.

steel or aluminium, with the exception of the 2mm - size where more flexible, coated steel needles are available, as well as bamboo and wood. However, sometimes, coated steel needles in sizes finer than 2mm can be found in secondhand shops or among family heirlooms.

The Shetland knitters used comparatively big needle sizes for their fine ring-shawls, in that most of them are knitted on 2.75mm needles and larger. However, there are smaller pieces knitted on very fine needles as illustrated by the example shown in Figure 18. The finest needles which can be purchased in Shetland for use in the knitting belt, as shown in Figure 17, are 1.75mm. (UK 16, US 00).

Figure 18. Shetland tray cloth by courtesy of the Lerwick Museum.

For making garments and articles designed so as to use the readily available, middle range of yarns there is generally a wide choice of needles. Whereas the use of unconventional materials may necessitate a search for alternative tools and it may even be necessary to improvise.

It is worthwhile to try as many different styles of knitting needle as possible, as it will soon be discovered that even the length of needles, flexibility, the type of finish, colour, shape of the points, and even the weight and size of the knobs, can all

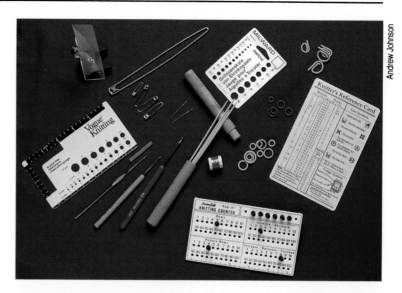

Figure 19. Knitting accessories.

Andrew Johnson

contribute to the comfort or otherwise of the individual knitter.

Also a good idea, is to make a collection of useful accessories which become available, especially as the range of projects and materials used is extended beyond the traditional. Figure 19. shows a variety of useful tools which can probably be classified as 'crutches' and 'lifesavers'! What is most important is to keep them in a place where you can find them in a hurry when you need them! Not to mention remembering you have them and trying them out.

For the sewing-up of projects, a range of tapestry needles, from very fine through to quite large, are essential as the rounded points of these needles allow edges to be 'laced' together without splitting the yarn, and there are times when they can also be very useful to reconstruct the knitted fabric when, due to a minor error, a repair or improvisation is required.

3. When is Lace Appropriate?

ॐ

Making decisions about yarns, needles and patterns

It is very difficult to explain what happens when expressing an idea which is spontaneous, one which has arisen from a sudden impulse, or natural feeling. Part of the inspiration has come from drawing on accumulated knowledge, whether obtained consciously or not, and also from making use of new discoveries which have occurred over a period of time. In creative terms this is true of whatever medium one is using.

For example, a painter starting out on a new work would not construct a typical 'painting by numbers' plan prior to putting paint on canvas and adding the appropriate colours and textures. In most cases the artist will have a 'general' idea of what is to be portrayed and may roughly sketch in the main elements as a guide to the finished work. Such a sketch can readily be abandoned should the work develop in different 'spontaneous' directions.

Next to my craft my other great love is drawing and painting, although I have no formal qualifications and the tuition I have received has been for very short periods during Summer Schools and short-term seminars. I feel that there is a definite parallel between the teaching I have received in these classes and the principles involved in creating lace in knitting. For this reason, I feel I can best express these underlying principles by using similar examples and exercises in my practical designing as those which have been exemplified in such teaching as I have received.

A piece of lace works well when the placement is such that the pattern can be seen and enjoyed against an appropriate background. The background for lace is often overlooked by the designer and in fact it is an integral part of the design, much like the artist's canvas. The success of a painting can be greatly enhanced by the choice of surface. It may be smooth or coarsely textured and even coloured. Similarly, with lace quite dramatic or subtle effects can be introduced simply by the choice of background.

Figures 20, 21, 22, 23 and 24 illustrate some examples of how this can happen. The first example (Figure 20) shows a contrasting, plain background which focuses the attention on the design of the lace. The second example (Figure 21) uses a background which is far more subtle and it is the texture of the lace, in contrast to the sheen of the silk over which it is draped, which is highlighted.

Figure 20. Lace mounted on dark background.

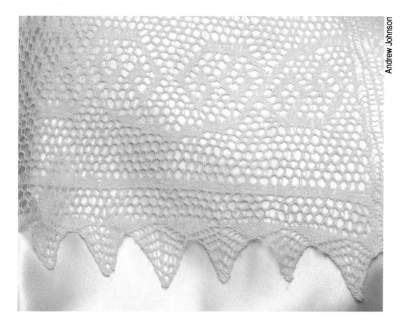

Figure 21. Lace over background reflecting light.

Figure 22. Above left: window without curtain. left: enhanced view with lace curtain.

The third example (Figure 22) shows how the view from the window is part of the total design. In this case the lace is used to frame the subject which is the climbing rose and repeats this motif in the design. The curtain is also shaped in such a way as to mask the less attractive aspects of the view.

An extension of this principle is shown in the fourth example (Figure 23) where strong shapes and 'busy' areas are taken into account and finally (Figure 24), a placement where light and background allow shadows to become part of the effect of the lace.

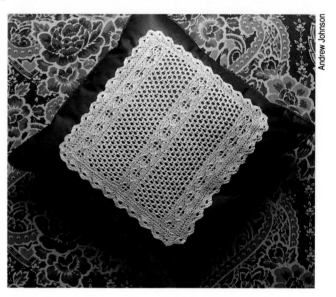

Figure 23. Lace designed for 'busy' background.

Figure 24. Shadows formed by lace.

One of the early exercises required in a drawing class is to make a 'value scale' from white to black and usually eight grey values as shown in Figure 25. A similar effect can be devised with lace if one regards the solid knitted areas as one end of the value scale and the holes or spaces as the other end. For this purpose the background needs to be a contrast to the colour of the yarn used as in Figure 26. The following exercises are designed to produce a series of knitted samples which allow varying amounts of the background to show through.

The instructions will be given in both written and chart form and, as well, each abbreviation will be accompanied by a written and graphic interpretation consistent with generally accepted knitting practice. See Appendix A.

The best way to look at a chart is to regard it as a drawing of the knitted fabric where each square represents a stitch. The front, or 'right side' of the work is facing the knitter and this is why the chart is read from the bottom right, unless the article is started from the back or 'wrong side'. This is indicated by the row numbers at the sides so that if the bottom row of squares is numbered '1' at the right-hand side then the first row is worked with the 'right side' of the work facing the knitter. If the number '1' is on the left-hand side of the chart then the first row is worked with the 'wrong side' of the work facing the knitter.

Figure 25. Value scale

Figure 26. Lace value scale.

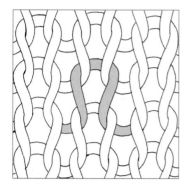

Figure 27. Knit fabric

Figure 28. Purl fabric

The symbols used to describe the way each of the stitches is to be worked are given as they appear on the right side of the work, which explains why stocking (US stockinette) stitch is shown with the squares of every row written to symbolise a knit stitch when this is achieved by the wrong-side row being purled! If you have knitted in the round, you will easily see how this works as, in this case, you do not purl the alternate rows, as when working on a straight piece, in order to obtain a smooth fabric.

When interpreting the methods shown to achieve the different stitch positions, I personally don't think it matters too much how the result is achieved, as long as it is a comfortable and efficient way for the knitter and the resulting position of the stitch or stitches involved match the diagram. So if the knitter is self-taught, a left-handed person or has some disability which requires using the knitting needles in a different way, then use whatever method achieves the required result in the way that is most suitable to make the craft a pleasure.

For the first series use plain stocking stitch of one row knit as in Figure 27, and one row purl as in Figure 28. These are shown on a chart as empty squares where the chart shows the right side of the fabric and as dots in the squares where the purl or reverse side of the fabric is shown. Figure 29. The abbreviation for stocking stitch is 'St st' or 'st st'. The abbreviation for knit is 'K' or 'k' and the abbreviation for purl is 'P' or 'p'. Further details of symbols and abbreviations can be found in Appendix A.

Unless directed otherwise, use the following methods for casting on and casting off (US bind off) as they allow for plenty of movement.

Figure 29. Stocking stitch and reverse stocking stitch.

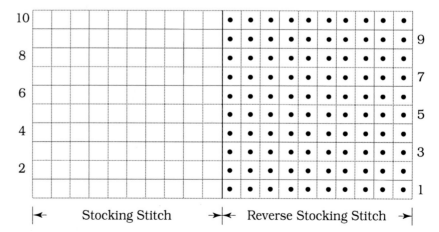

The casting on method is described as a *knitting on* in most books. Begin by making a half hitch as shown in Figure 30 for the first stitch then, using the second needle, place it in the front of the first loop and bring the yarn over the right-hand needle as shown in Figure 31, drawing it through the loop of the first stitch. Place this new loop on the left-hand needle beside the first, being careful not to twist it. Repeat until the desired number of stitches are on the left-hand needle. Knit one row into the front of the loops as shown in Figure 32. Unless otherwise stated, all knit stitches are to be made by knitting into the front, or near side of the loop as shown in Figure 32.

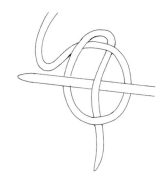

Figure 30. Making a half hitch.

To cast off. K2, * put both stitches back on to left-hand needle and k2 tog, k1, repeat from * until all stitches are worked off. Use normal knitting tension.

Use the same yarn for all the exercises so that comparisons can be made. A 50g ball (2oz) of a 4-ply, fine Double Knit or Fingering weight yarn of approximately 36 wraps per 5cms (18 wraps per inch) is recommended.

Sample 1a With size 2mm needles (UK 14, US 00) cast on 25 stitches and work 26 rows then cast off.

Sample 2a With size 4mm needles (UK 8, US 6) cast on 20 stitches and work 20 rows then cast off.

Sample 3a With size 5mm needles (UK 6, US 8) cast on 16 stitches and work 16 rows then cast off.

Wash and block each sample in the following manner: wash the sample in warm water with a mild soap or detergent and remove excess moisture in a towel. While still damp, pin into shape with sufficient tension to give the stitches definition. Steam lightly and leave to dry.

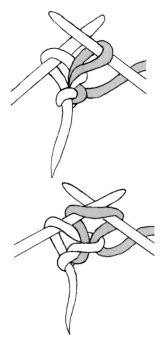

Figure 31. Knitting on.

Repeat this exercise using a much finer yarn and the same three sets of needles. It will now be obvious that, as the size of the needle increases, the amount of background showing through also increases. Figure 33.

It becomes easy to see that the larger the needle size in relation to fine wool the 'lacier' it becomes and that with thick wool the needles need to be very large to achieve a similar effect. This latter discovery explains why, as it became increasingly more difficult to obtain fine Shetland and lace weight yarns in wool, many shawl patterns which use 3- and 4-ply baby wools are knitted on large needles. Until recently, those of us who want patterns on very fine needles for lace shawls, have needed to raid collections of very old knitting books printed when fine

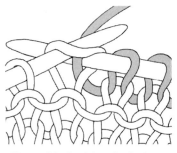

Figure 32. Position for knit.

*Figure 33.
Stocking stitch
value scale,
made from
samples 1a, 2a
and 3a.*

*Figure 34.
Stocking
stitch value
scale in
cotton.*

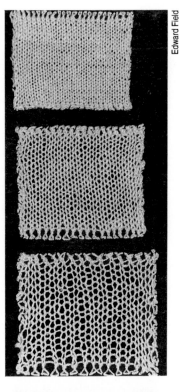

*Figure 35.
Stocking stitch
value scale in
rayon.*

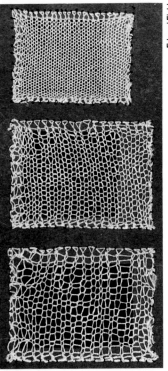

*Figure 36.
Stocking stitch
value scale in
silk.*

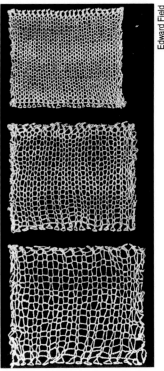

yarns were available or, resort to using table cloth patterns designed to be knitted in crochet cotton.

To complete this exercise, work further samples using yarns with different properties, for example cotton, linen, viscose and compare the results. Figures 34, 35 and 36.

A 'value' scale has now been produced by using a plain fabric and varying grist and needle size. The next stage is to use holes to give a similar effect.

Using size 4mm (UK 8, US 6) work on the following series of three samples which will also introduce five new chart symbols.

The first of these is a 'yarn over' and is worked as shown in Figure 37. It is shown on the chart as $\boxed{O}$ and the abbreviation used is 'Yo' or 'yo'. On the following row a yarn over is worked as a regular stitch unless special instructions are given, so resist the temptation to put a twist into it by working into the back of the loop!

The second is 'make one' by picking up and knitting the thread between the last worked stitch on the right-hand needle and the next stitch on the left-hand needle as shown in Figure 38. It is shown on the chart as $\boxed{M}$ and the abbreviation used is 'M1' or 'm1'.

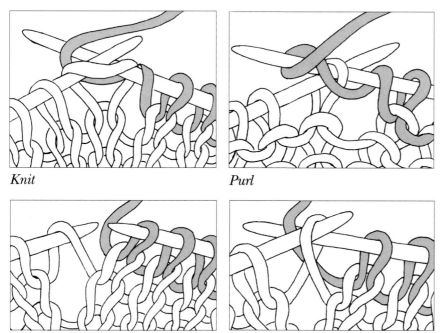

Knit

Purl

Figure 37. Making a yarn over.

Stage 1

Stage 2

Figure 38. Working a make one.

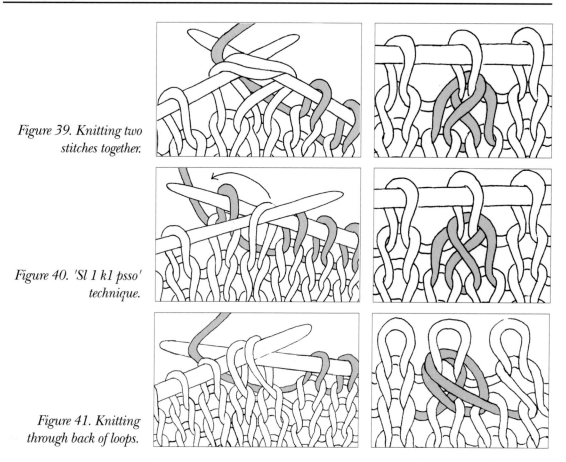

Figure 39. Knitting two stitches together.

Figure 40. 'Sl 1 k1 psso' technique.

Figure 41. Knitting through back of loops.

The third is 'knit two stitches together' as shown in Figure 39. It is shown on the chart as ☐ and the abbreviation used is 'K2 tog' or 'k2 tog'.

The fourth is another method of decreasing which slants in the other direction. It can be worked by slipping the first stitch then knitting the next stitch and completed by passing the slipped stitch over the knitted stitch as shown in Figure 40. The chart symbol is ☐ and the abbreviation is 'Sl 1 k1 psso' or 'sl 1 k1 psso'.

An alternative method of obtaining this result is described later in Chapter 4 and illustrated in Figure 59.

The fifth is to change the direction of the stitch by working it 'through the back of the loop' as shown in Figure 41. The chart symbol is B and the abbreviation is 'tbl'.

The use of p2 tog tbl creates a wrong side version of sl 1 k1 psso. However, working through the back of the stitches also twists them which means k2 tog tbl, is not a mirror image of k2 tog.

Sample 1b

Cast on 20 sts and work two rows in st st.

Row 1. K3,* yo, sl 1, k1, psso. Repeat from * to last 3 sts, k3.
Row 2. P4,* p1 tbl, p1. Repeat from * to last 2 sts, p2.
Row 3. K4,* yo, sl 1, k1, psso. Repeat from * to last 2 sts, k2.
Row 4. P3,* p1 tbl, p1. Repeat from * to last 3 sts, p3.
Repeat these four rows twice more.
Row 13. K2,* k2 tog, yo. Repeat from * to last 4 sts, k4.
Row 14. As row 2.
Row 15. K3,* k2 tog, yo. Repeat from * to last 3 sts, k3.
Row 16. As row 4.
Repeat last four rows twice more.
Row 25. As row 1.
Row 26. As row 2.
Row 27. As row 15.
Row 28. As row 4.
Repeat these four rows twice more then work two rows st st and
and cast off.

Figure 42. Chart for Sample 1b.

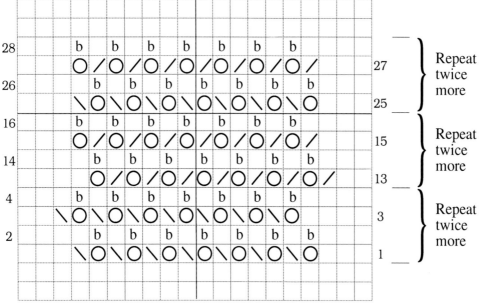

37

Sample 2b

Cast on 20 sts and work 2 rows in st st.

Row 1. K3,* m1, sl 1, k1, psso. Repeat from * to last 3 sts, k3.
Rows 2 and **4.** Purl.
Row 3. K2,* m1, sl 1, k1, psso. Repeat to last 2 sts, k2.
Repeat twice more.
Row 13. K3,* k2 tog, m1. Repeat from * to last 3 sts, k3.
Row 14 and **16.** Purl.
Row 15. K2,* k2 tog, m1. Repeat from * to last 2 sts, k2.
Repeat last four rows twice more.
Row 25. As row 3.
Rows 26 and **28.** Purl.
Row 27. As row 15.
Repeat last four rows twice more then work two rows st st and
cast off.

Figure 43. Chart for Sample 2b.

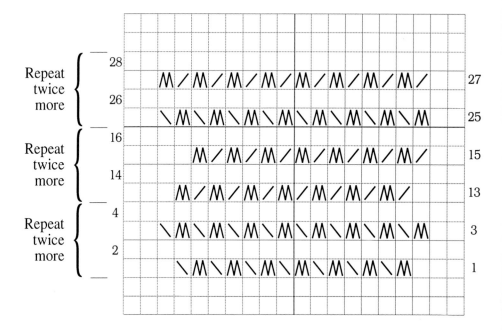

Sample 3b

Cast on 20 sts and work two rows in st st.

Row 1. K3,* yo, sl 1, k1, psso. Repeat from * to last 3 sts k3.
Rows 2 and **4.** Purl.
Row 3. K4,* yo, sl 1, k1, psso. Repeat from * to last 2 sts k2.
Repeat twice more.
Row 13. K2,* k2 tog, yo. Repeat from * to last 4 sts, k4.
Rows 14 and **16.** Purl.
Row 15. K3,* k2 tog, yo. Repeat from * to last 3 sts, k3.
Repeat last four rows twice more.
Row 25. As row 1.
Rows 26 and **28.** Purl.
Row 27. As row 15.
Repeat last four rows twice more then work two rows st st and
cast off.

Figure 44. Chart for Sample 3b.

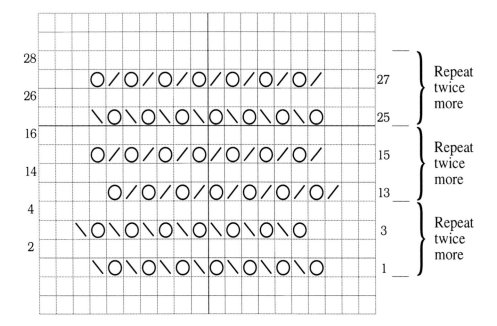

Sample 4b

Using the same yarn and needles as used for the first three samples, cast on 20 sts and knit two rows in st st.

Row 1. K1,* yo, k2 tog. Repeat from * to last st, k1. Repeat this row 9 times.

Row 11. K1,* yo, sl 1, k1, psso. Repeat from * to last st, k1. Repeat this row 9 times.

Row 21. K1,* yo, p2 tog. Repeat from * to last st, k1. Repeat this row 9 times then work two rows st st and cast off.

Figure 45. Chart for Sample 4b.

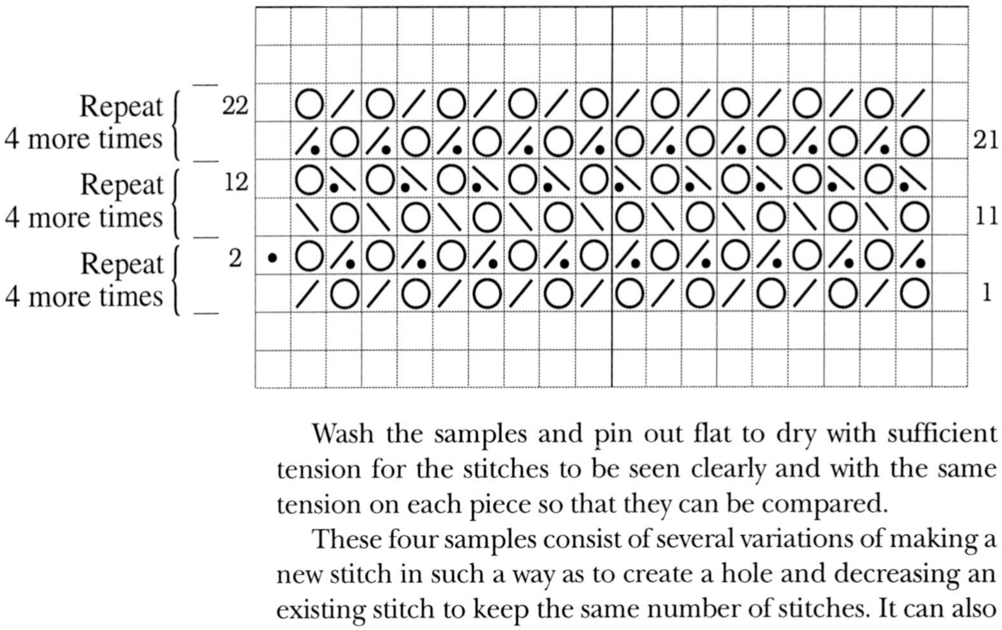

Repeat 4 more times { 22 / 21
Repeat 4 more times { 12 / 11
Repeat 4 more times { 2 / 1

Wash the samples and pin out flat to dry with sufficient tension for the stitches to be seen clearly and with the same tension on each piece so that they can be compared.

These four samples consist of several variations of making a new stitch in such a way as to create a hole and decreasing an existing stitch to keep the same number of stitches. It can also be seen that some unexpected traps can occur for the unwary. In samples **1a, 2a and 3a**, a row of plain knitting is worked between each row of holes, a bias is created where the decreases are always made on the same side of the made stitch. The third variation of each of these three samples shows how this can be corrected by alternating the position of the decrease. In sample **4a** the bias does not occur as the made stitch is on the other side of the decrease on the alternate row. Figures 46 and 47.

This bias effect can be used to make a zigzag edging by filling in the space created by the bias as shown in Figures 48 and 49. It is interesting to note that this is one of the occasions when the chart may not illustrate the appearance of the knitting, as the zigzag effect is actually seen on the other side from where it appears in the knitting. However, this can be drawn, as shown

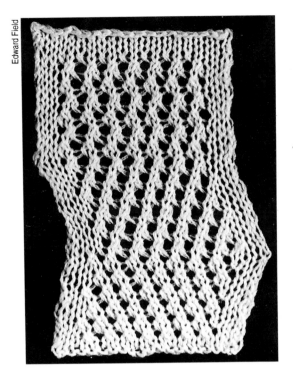

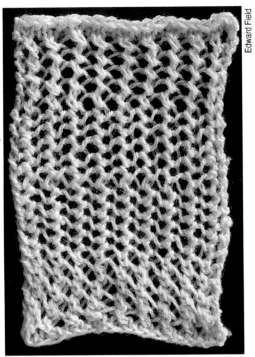

Figure 46. Bias effect on Sample 1b.

Figure 47. Sample 4b.

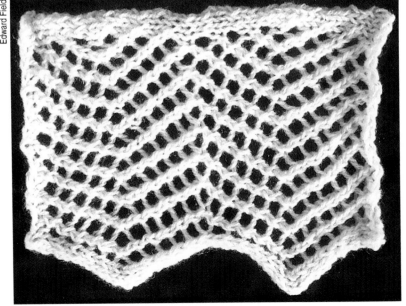

Figure 48. Sample showing edging using natural bias.

Figure 49. Chart for Figure 48.

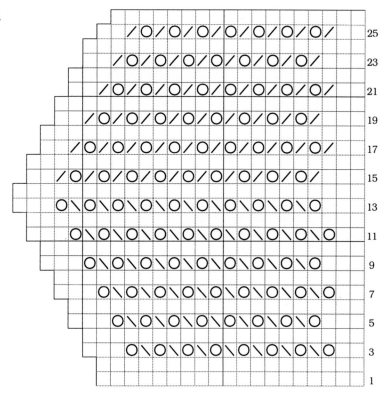

in Figure 50, which gives a visually accurate version of the finished appearance.

Another important observation to make at this stage is the difference in width of each sample, depending on the method used to make the holes. In comparison with a new stitch being made by making a loop over the needle which is later knitted as an ordinary stitch, we can see a major difference when the loop is lifted from the row below and this is further accentuated when a made loop is knitted through the back, thus introducing a twist which not only makes the hole smaller but draws the fabric together even more. It is important to be aware of such effects when using these stitches in your own design, as the variations will need to be taken into account in order to keep the size and shape of the article correct. These effects can also be useful little tricks to be remembered and applied when shaping articles and for when one reaches the stage of inventing entirely new variations and motifs.

The next exercise is to repeat some of the above using other yarns made from other fibres, for example cotton, silk and

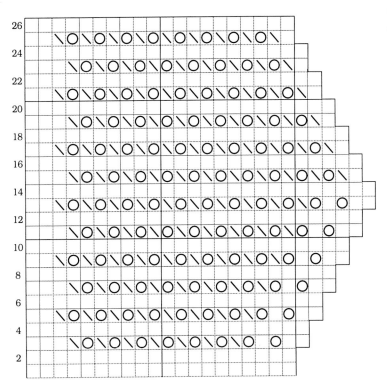

Figure 50. Alternative chart for Figure 48.

synthetics, as well as fibres which have a 'halo' of fibre like angora and mohair. The difference in elasticity and the smoothness, or otherwise, of these yarns will introduce further variations which are useful to note.

For example, notice the effects which are created by sheen on the yarn, especially when combinations are used as shown in Figure 16, page 22. One of the special properties of fibres like angora is the extra warmth created by trapping air around the fibres, and open stitch designs can provide a creative as well as an effective way of doing this.

Very slippery yarns, like rayon when used on its own as shown in Figure 35, change the appearance of a pattern due to the movement of the yarn and, if knitted again in a soft cotton, as in Figure 34, there is a noticeable difference in the size of the holes in relation to the rest of the fabric as it 'sticks' together.

The lustre, or ability to reflect light of some of these yarns, will also accentuate such details as the line created by the stitches which have been worked together. If mounted on a dull or textured background, this can create a contrast which adds another element to a design.

You may also wish to make a series of graded samples, as shown in Figure 51, by repeating the parts of the above exercises which give examples without a bias of various densities, thus giving a range of values. Those illustrated were made by casting on 20 sts and working 2 rows st st before starting the pattern and again after completing 20 rows of the pattern. Extend this scale with your own choice of patterns. You will note that patterns 2 and 3 in Figure 51 need to change places.

To make a value scale using different size needles similar to the one shown in Figure 52, cast on 20 sts and work the chosen patterns, dividing each change with four rows of plain knitting. The result will be wider at the top than at the cast-on edge. After blocking, run a coloured thread from each end of the cast-on edge in a straight line to the cast-off edge as shown in Figure 53. Where each pattern and needle change occurs, count the number of stitches between the coloured threads and then re-knit the sample, decreasing evenly across the row to that number of stitches on the row before the needle change.

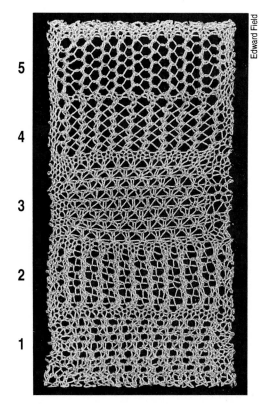

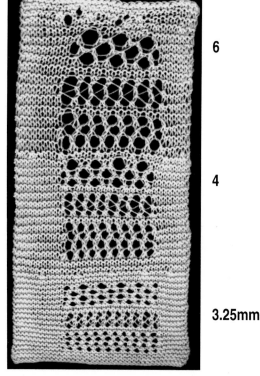

Figure 51. Value scale using one size of needles.   *Figure 52. Value scale using needles of different sizes.*

44

When evaluating all these samples, bear in mind other qualities, in particular the differences in elasticity when comparing one pattern with another worked on the same size needle, as well as those worked on the larger needles, and make relevant notes.

After washing and blocking, mount all samples, preferably so that both sides can be seen. Heavy card with a square removed with a craft knife is ideal, or samples encased in plastic and one side mounted on card, is another possible solution. Figures 54 and 55.

Store in a ring binder or folder which allows the cards of samples to be removed when required as it is a hindrance to have a bulky, heavy folder to pick up every time you want to work with only one or two patterns.

Continue to extend this resource by adding new patterns which you like or feel could be useful. It can be really helpful to have a variety of patterns giving similar density which are constructed in different ways. This gives plenty of choice and enables you to select a pattern when one is needed to work in harmony with other patterns in a particular piece.

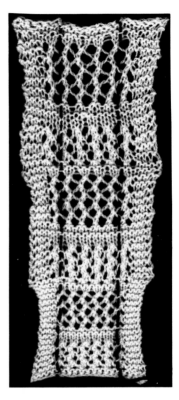

Figure 53. Coloured threads to show stitch numbers.

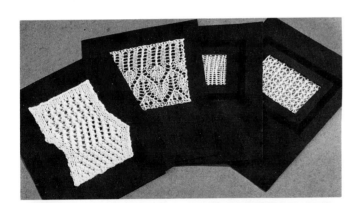

Figure 54. Samples mounted on card.

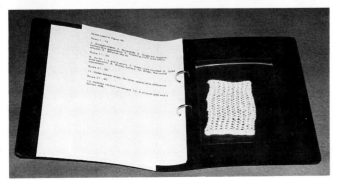

Figure 55. Samples mounted in plastic.

45

4. Cause and Effect with Stitches

汐

Exercises to extend proficiency and to make decisions

In the samples produced in the previous chapter it will be noted that the surface texture varies depending on how the stitches are worked. Even the thickness of the fabric is affected and this can be changed yet again if the fabric is relaxed, compared with when it is under tension. The amount of tension which is introduced at the time of blocking the fabric is decided by the end use of the fabric. Consequently, very fine, open lace designs will look even lacier if blocked out with considerable tension, however, a yarn like angora, where three-dimensional 'pockets' are the aim, the reverse is desired and the finished piece should be eased into shape with minimal tension.

The surface texture which is created by the method used for decreasing can be changed by choosing a different direction for the stitches to lie which have been knitted together. For example, by interchanging knit two together for knit one, slip one, pass the slipped stitch over and vice versa, the raised ridges, or chains, as shown on the right of Figure 56, formed by the decreases are eliminated thus giving a smoother surface as shown to the left of the sample in Figure 56.

This ability to use the decreases to create a surface effect

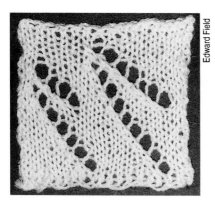

Figure 56. Smooth fabric decrease..

Figure 57. Use of decrease to define patterns.

can be used to great advantage as part of a design, especially where a shape is to be defined or emphasised, and can often be strategically placed for this very purpose. Figure 57 shows an example of this technique. Increases can be used decoratively. The increase used in this sample 1(c) is made by knitting first into the front of the stitch and then into the back of the same stitch before slipping it off the left-hand needle. Figure 58, here the chart symbol is $\boxed{B}$ and the abbreviation used is 'incB'.

The abbreviation 'ssk' has been introduced for the next set of samples as an alternative to 'sl 1, k1, psso'. It is shown on the chart with the same symbol as the direction in which the stitches lie is the same. It is achieved by slipping two stitches from the left-hand needle, one at a time, by placing the right-hand needle into the front of the stitch and then sliding the left-hand needle into the back of both stitches and knitting them together as shown in Figure 59. This may be a speedier method for some knitters and is less awkward to do than it is to describe.

To work a purled decrease through the back of the stitches can often be very slow and awkward, and the same result can be achieved if the first stitch of the decrease is purled in the usual manner and then placed back on the left-hand needle where the next stitch is slipped over it without working it. The stitch is now returned to the right-hand needle. This is shown as the abbreviation 'p2 tog tbl' and the symbol on the chart as $\boxed{\diagdown}$.

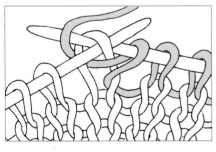

Knit

Purl

Figure 58. Increasing in front and back of loop.

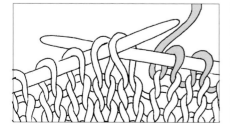

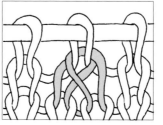

Figure 59. Slip, slip knit.

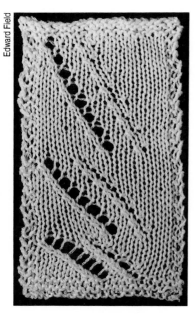

Edward Field

Figure 60. Sample of angles formed by increases and decreases.

Sample 1c

Cast on 20 stitches using the yarn used in the first set of samples and needle size 4mm (UK 8, US 6), and work four foundation rows in garter stitch. Continue as follows.

Row 1. K4, incB, ssk, k2, yo, ssk, k9.
Row 2. K2, p6, p2 tog tbl, yo, p2, p2 tog tbl, incB, p3, k2.
Row 3. K6, incB, ssk, k2, yo, ssk, k7.
Row 4. K2, p4, p2 tog tbl, yo, p2, p2 tog tbl, incB, p5, k2.
Row 5. K8, incB, ssk, k2, yo, ssk, k5.
Row 6. K2, p2, p2 tog tbl, yo, p2, p2 tog tbl, incB, p7, k2.
Row 7. K10, incB, ssk, k2, yo, ssk, k3.
Row 8. K2, p2 tog tbl, yo, p2, p2 tog tbl, incB, p9, k2.
Row 9. As row 1.
Row 10 and **following alternate rows.** K2, p16, k2.
Row 11. K5, incB, ssk, k2, yo, ssk, k8.
Row 13. As row 3.
Row 15. k7, incB, ssk, k2, yo, ssk, k6.
Row 17. As row 5.
Row 19. K9, incB, ssk, k2, yo, ssk, k4.
Row 21. As row 7.
Row 23. K11, incB, ssk, k2, yo, ssk, k2.

Complete the sample by repeating row 1 and decreasing every third row and note the change in the angle of the line created by the decreases. Figures 60 and 61.

Another way to change the surface texture is to use a garter stitch (every row knit) base. Although this creates ridges on both sides of the work, it can also have the effect of 'flattening' the pattern. Figure 62.

I find that although the ridges formed by the decreases, which are so clearly defined in stocking stitch, do not show in garter stitch, there is a difference in the way the stitches lie in relation to the neighbouring stitches and the appearance of the eyelet if it is adjacent to the decrease to justify being selective as to when to decrease through the back of the loops and when to choose the front of the loops.

Garter stitch is often used as a base for shawls and for when the article is to be reversible. Garter stitch blocks out very successfully for lace patterns which are to be finished under tension. Figure 63.

The edges also stay flat when worked in garter stitch, unlike stocking stitch which tends to curl, and garter stitch also has an advantage when used with yarns where the twist is not balanced,

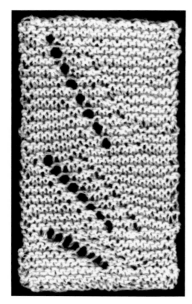

Figure 62. Garter stitch version of sample 1c.

Figure 61. Chart of Figure 60.

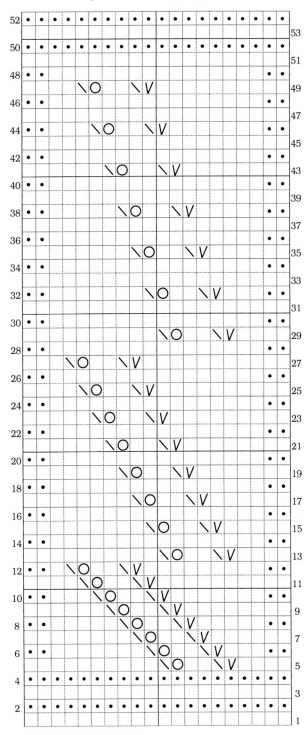

Figure 63. Garter stitch shawl.

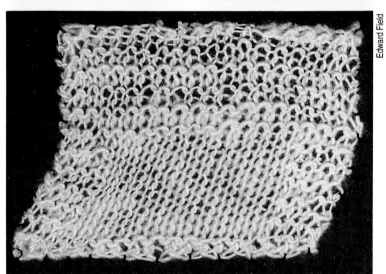

Figure 64. Unbalanced yarn causing bias over stocking stitch and corrected by using garter stitch.

in that it corrects the tendency to form a bias, as shown in the stocking stitch and garter stitch samples in Figure 64. It also takes fewer stitches and more rows to measure the same size as stocking stitch which is knitted using the same yarn and needle-size. However, it has considerable stretch and for some projects a smaller needle size may be necessary to control this tendency.

Work the sample 3(b) in garter stitch and note the differences described above. Figure 65.

When planning a project, consideration must be given to the effect the final blocking of the article will have on the pattern. It would obviously not be appropriate to have areas of the article worked in a pattern which is to be blocked under

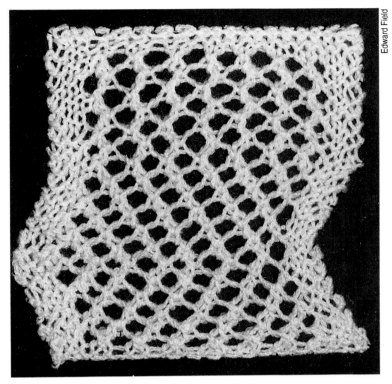

Figure 65. Sample 3b in garter stitch.

Figure 66. Chart for Figure 65.

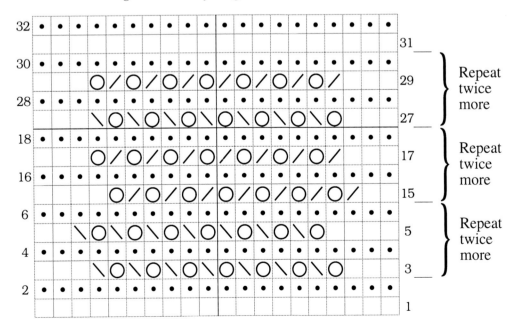

51

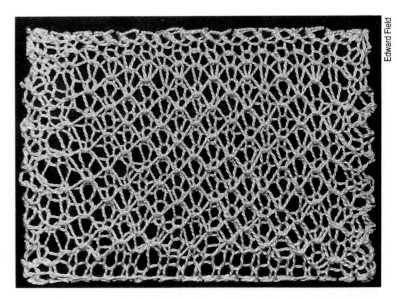

Edward Field

Figure 67. Brioche stitch.

tension coming in close proximity to a pattern which relies on the stitches being in a relaxed position to accentuate the raised areas and ridges. However, it is also possible to use the final blocking process to 'coax' patterns to produce special effects.

This leads to the exploration of patterns which are traditionally not lace at all, for example, Fisherman's Rib. By using the knowledge gained from the initial exercises in Chapter 3, these patterns can be used very successfully in lace designs and can increase the range of background stitches, so providing special effects and saving a great deal of time.

An example of this first use would be that of gaining an overall, often reversible, effect of lace without the ridges, surface texture and dense areas which result from lace fabric where the holes are made by either the 'make one' or 'yarn over' method together with an associated decrease to balance the number of stitches. Figure 67.

An example of the second use is illustrated in the construction of the sleeve shown in Figure 68, where a combination of lace knitted on fine needles and fine yarn has been combined with a lace effect obtained by using the same yarn but considerably larger size needles. At the edge, the rib pattern is blocked flat and under tension, however where it is next to the fine insertion, the rib is drawn together to give the effect of fine pleating.

There are several of these patterns which are useful to the knitter of lace as a means of achieving effects quickly and simply in a design. As discussed earlier in Chapter Two, there are times when it is necessary to make a decision about the amount of time which is available and appropriate for a project. Using 'large-needle' areas, which provide a background for attention to be focused on the more significant and detailed areas of the design, can often be even more successful than painstakingly executing these areas on very fine needles.

These stitches also provide a mesh which looks well with knitted lace patterns by matching the single thread which separates each hole. Figure 69.

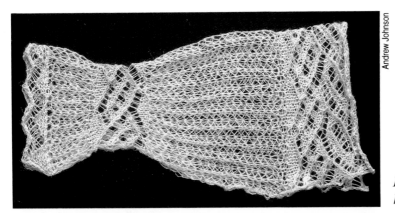

Figure 68. Sleeve showing lace knitting used with rib.

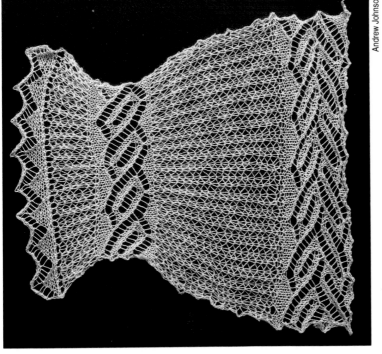

Figure 69. Detail of Figure 68 showing how the shaping is affected by the change in needle size.

53

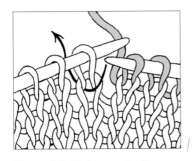

Figure 70. Fisherman's rib technique.

Use a fine yarn, such as a lace-weight wool or No. 20 crochet cotton, and choose a needle size to give a very open effect similar to that achieved in sample 3(a) in Chapter Three.

Fisherman's Rib introduces a new technique which requires the stitch of the previous row to be knitted as shown in Figure 70. This is shown on the chart as ↓.

Sample 2(c)

Fisherman's Rib

Cast on 20 sts and knit two rows in garter stitch.

Pattern row. K2,* k1, k1 in the row below. Repeat from * to last 2 sts. K2. Repeat this row nineteen times.

Last row of pattern. K2,* p1, k1 in the row below. Repeat from * to last 2 sts. K2.

Work two rows of garter stitch and cast off. Figure 70.

A similar effect can be achieved by using Brioche stitch. Although a 'yarn over' is used in this pattern, it is used to create a different result from eyelet, faggotting or trellis patterns as worked earlier.

Figure 71a. Chart for Sample 2(c).

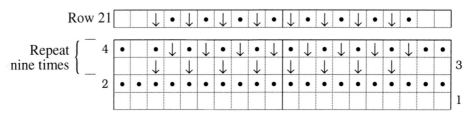

Sample 3(c)

Double Brioche or Honeycomb Stitch

Cast on 20 sts and knit two rows garter stitch.

Row 1. (wrong side) k2,* k1, yo, sl 1. Repeat from * to last 2 sts. K2.

Row 2. K3,* sl the yo st, k2. Repeat from * to last st. K1.

Row 3. K2,* yo, sl 1, k2 tog—(ie yo of previous row and next stitch). Repeat from * to last 2 sts. K2.

Row 4. K2,* k2, sl yo st. Repeat from * to last 2 sts. K2.

Row 5. K2,* k2 tog—(ie yo of previous row and next stitch)— yo, sl 1. Repeat from * to last 2 sts. K2.

Row 6. K3,* sl yo st, k2. Repeat from * to last st. K1.

Repeat rows 3—6 inclusive four more times.

Knit one row knitting 'yarn over' of previous row together with adjacent stitch. Knit one more row and cast off.

Figure 71b. Chart for Sample 3(c).

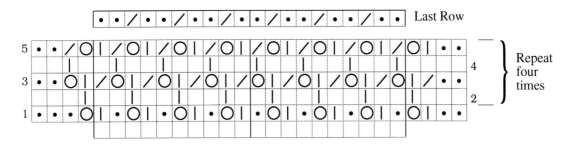

Sample 4(c)

Rib

Cast on 20 sts and knit two rows in garter stitch.

Work 20 rows in k1, p1, rib at the same time knitting two stitches at each end of every row in garter stitch to make a border. Work two rows in garter stitch and cast off.

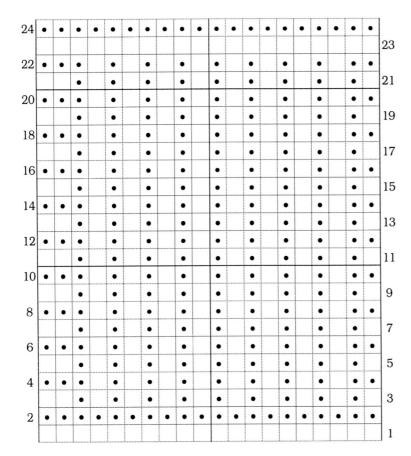

Figure 72. Chart for Sample 4(c).

Figure 73. Mounted samples.

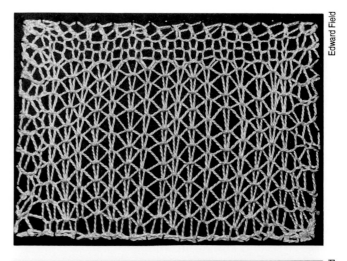

Sample 2(c)

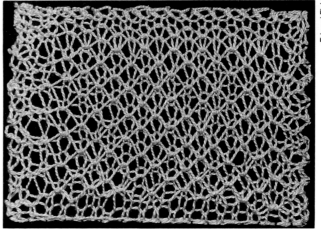

Sample 3(c)

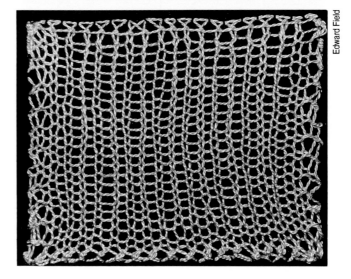

Sample 4(c)

Wash and block samples and mount. Figure 73.

It will be noted that samples 2(c) and 3(c) are patterns where because of knitting into the row below in 2(c) and the slipped stitches in 3(c) it is necessary to complete two rows to achieve the depth of one row. Experiment with other similar patterns and evaluate them, noting any particular characteristics they may have and the occasions when these could be advantageous or otherwise.

As a last sample for this series of exercises there is a technique which it is useful to know when designing reversible patterns which have areas of stocking stitch. As with 2(c) and 3(c) above, this needs to be used with discretion as it also takes two rows to achieve the depth of one row. However, if this is a problem, then techniques such as 'short rows' which will be described later, can be employed.

The method of slipping the stitch in this pattern is shown in Figure 74. It is described as 'slip 1 with yarn in front'. The abbreviation is 'sl 1 wyif' and it is shown on the chart as $\boxed{-}$.

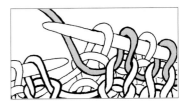

Figure 74. Slip one with yarn in front.

Sample 5(c)

Use needle size 4mm (UK 8, US 6) and the yarn used for the first samples.

Cast on 20 sts and work two rows in garter stitch.

Foundation row. Knit into the front and back of each stitch.

Row 1. K1, sl 1 wyif, repeat to end of row.

Repeat this row 37 times more.

Next row. K2 tog to end.

Knit one more row and cast off. Figure 75.

This technique will be referred to as 'double knitting' because of the space which is created between the front and the back of the fabric and it will be referred to in later chapters on several occasions as it can provide a very professional finish for welts, casings, edgings and special effects such as ruching.

All the exercises up to this point have covered very basic knitting techniques in order to build up a common vocabulary of terms, abbreviations and a system of showing these

Figure 75. Chart for double stocking stitch, Sample 5(c).

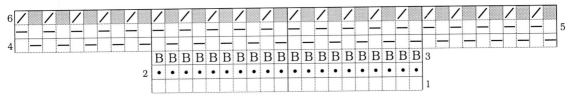

movements graphically by using symbols on a chart. Before moving into more specific study of the structure of knitted fabric the reasons for the terms and symbols chosen for this text will be discussed.

Over the years I have been amazed at the variety of terms and symbols used to describe knitting techniques. With the increased availability of patterns from other countries this can cause a great deal of confusion. Teaching workshops also highlight the diversity of terms and meanings. Even after careful research, there are always new 'gremlins' to thwart an otherwise well-planned programme! However, from a more positive point of view, evaluating these terms can also add to one's knowledge and appreciation of the evolution of the structure of knitted fabric.

To ensure that the terms and abbreviations selected to be used in this book are clearly understood as each one is introduced, it is accompanied by a diagram to illustrate the construction and position of the stitches required. There are also suggestions as to how this may be accomplished, however, as there are so many different ways of achieving even the simplest of manipulations, knitters should be aware first of all of the end result and then concern themselves with adopting the most comfortable method to suit them.

During my research for Chapter 1 I enjoyed testing out instructions from many publications and one of the most interesting projects was from a book called *Treasures in Needlework* first published in 1870. The authors were Mrs Warren and Mrs Pullman and the relevant chapter is titled, 'Workable Patterns— Plain and Practical Instructions'.

I chose to try out the lace motif for a knitted curtain on page 61. Materials and needle size were given, however, there was no information on tension or information about the finished size of the curtain which meant it was not possible to decide whether the needle size given was that used in British or American sizing. However, because of the date of the pattern, I assumed it to be the British size.

The number of stitches for each motif was given, in this case 38 with a border of 10 stitches in plain knitting on each side of the piece.

Whereas in modern patterns the abbreviations, or a reference to where the abbreviations may be found are given, this was not provided and it was not until after I had puzzled out a solution, by trial and error, that I found a description of the techniques and abbreviations used, with illustrations included, on pages 59 to 61. The knitting patterns on the preceding pages did not refer to this abbreviation reference either, and another notable point is that on page 25 a pattern for a baby's knitted sock has the instructions written in full with no abbreviations at all! In these instructions 'purl' is spelled 'pearl' and yet in the instructions on pages 60 and 61, the spelling is 'purl'.

As I knitted the sample I also made a chart. This proved to be very helpful as there were several mistakes in the last few rows of the pattern which were indicated very quickly on the chart. The other really interesting point, concerning the instructions, was that there was no suggestion of reversing the position of the stitches in the decreases to make each half of the pattern a mirror image of the other. Maybe this was left to the knitter, however I doubt this as a sample of the pattern would need to be knitted for the knitter to decide where the adjustments to the instructions would need to be made. It must therefore be concluded that the instructions, compared with those expected by knitters today, were quite unsophisticated.

Having completed the chart, I made the alterations I decided were necessary to produce a symmetrical version which I then knitted. Figures 76 and 77 show the completed chart and an excerpt of the instructions. Figure 78 shows the result of the exercise before and after washing and blocking. Figure 79 shows the result compared with the illustration provided with the instructions.

This pattern appears to be an original design. There are several in this book which also appear to be original, the rest use earlier known patterns in different forms, for example, 'Old Shale'.

As the need for more specific instructions arose, authors of patterns working independently of each other, were bound to come up with different versions of expressing the same technique and there were times when the same, or similar, terms were used which had different meanings. A classic example of this is the use of the term to 'make one'.

This can be a real trap for the experienced knitter who does not check the key to abbreviations provided in each pattern publication before beginning a knitted project. In both old and new publications 'make one' can have the meaning described in Figure 37, or the meaning described for 'yarn over' illustrated in Figure 38.

Figure 76. Chart for 1856 curtain.

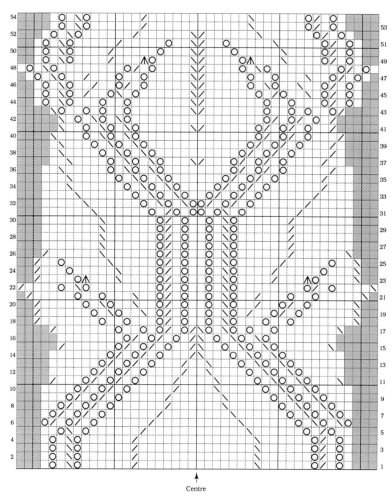

Centre

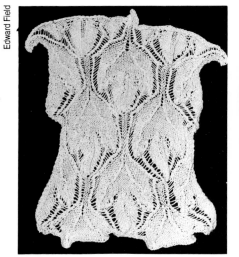

Figure 78. Comparison of unblocked (left) and blocked (right) knitted samples. Sample on right also shows symmetrical shaping above line of dark thread.

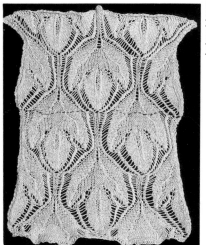

Edward Field

Andrew Johnson

60

KNITTED PATTERN FOR CURTAINS.   129

3 chain, 5 L *under* same, 5 L *under* the chains at point of leaf; 3 chain, 5 more L *under* same, 5 L *under* the 3 chain, Dc *under* same, Dc into same loop where commenced; * 3 chain, Dc into 3rd loop, 3 chain, Dc into 3rd loop, 3 chain, Dc into 3rd loop.

2nd Leaf.—12 chain, and work exactly the same as the last, but uniting after the 1st 5 L, into the 3rd L of last leaf; then *repeat* from * until the long stitches are reached, then work the same until 12 Leaves are made; then make 8 Leaves with only 2 chains of 3 between each Leaf (*this is round the corner*). Now work down the side as before.

The number of Leaves, that is, one more or less, is immaterial.

After washing, the D'Oyley should be pulled quite flat, and laid to press between linen, without stiffening, with a heavy weight upon it.

————

KNITTED PATTERN FOR CURTAINS.

No. 4 Evans's Boar's Head Cotton; No. 12 Pins.

Thirty eight stitches form one Pattern.

Cast on 400 stitches; this will make ten patterns, and ten stitches each side must be knitted plain at the commencement and end of each row.

1st Row.—K 1, Tf. K 1. K 2 +, Tf, K 6, K 2 +, K 14. K 2 +, K 6, Tf, K 2 +, K 1, Tf, K 1, *repeat* to the end.

2nd Row.—P 1, Tf, P 1, P 2 +, Tf, P 6, P 2 +, P 14, P 2 +, P 6, Tf, P 2 +, P 1, Tf, P 1.

3rd Row.—Same as 1st.

4th Row.—Same as 2nd.

5th Row.—Tf, K 2, Tf, K 2 +, K 1, Tf, K 6, K 2 +, K 12, K 2 +, K 6, Tf, K 1, K 2 +, Tf, K 2.

6th Row.—Tf, P 2 +, P 1, Tf, P 2 +, P 1, Tf, P 6, P 2 +, P 10, P 2 +, P 6, Tf, P 1, P 2 +, Tf, P 1, P 2 +, Tf, P 1.

7th Row.—K 2, Tf, K 2 +, K 1, Tf, K 2 +, K 1, Tf, K 6, K 2 +, K 8, K 2 +, K 6, Tf, K 1, K 2 +, Tf, K 1, K 2 +, Tf, K 1.

8th Row.—P 2, Tf, P 2 +, P 1, Tf, P 2 +, P 1, Tf, P 6, P 2 +, P 6, P 2 +, P 6, Tf, P 1, P 2 +, Tf, P 1, P 2 +, Tf, P 3.

9th Row.—K 4, Tf, K 2 +, K 1, Tf, K 2 +, K 1, Tf, K 5, K 2 +, K 6, K 2 +, K 5, Tf, K 1, K 2 +, Tf, K 1, K 2 +, Tf, K 3.

10th Row.—P 4, Tf, P 2 +, P 1, Tf, P 2 +, P 1, Tf, P 5, P 2 +, P 4, P 2 +, P 5, Tf, P 1, P 2 +, Tf, P 1, P 2 +, Tf, P 5.

11th Row.—K 1, K 2 +, K 3, Tf, K 2 +, K 1, Tf, K 2 +, K 1, Tf, K 4, K 2 +, K 4, K 2 +, K 4, Tf, K 1, K 2 +, Tf, K 1, K 2 +, Tf, K 3, K 2 +.

12th Row.—P 5, Tf, P 2 +, P 1, Tf, P 2 +, P 1, Tf, P 4, P 2 +, P 2, P 2 ᴠ, P 4, Tf, P 1, P 2 +, Tf, P 1, P 2 +, Tf, P 6.

13th Row.—K 7, Tf, K 2 +, K 1, Tf, K 2 +, K 1, Tf, K 3, K 2 +, K 2, K 2 +, K 3, Tf, K 1, K 2 +, Tf, K 1, K 2 +, Tf, K 6.

14th Row.—P 7, Tf, P 2 +, P 1, Tf, P 2 +, P 1, Tf, P 3, P 2 +, P 2 +, P 3, Tf, P 1, P 2 +, Tf, P 1, P 2 +, Tf, P 8.

15th Row.—K 1, K 2 +, K 6, Tf, K 2 +, K 1, Tf, K 2 +, K 1, Tf, K 2, K 2 +, K 2, Tf, K 1, K 2 +, Tf, K 1, K 2 +, Tf, K 6, K 2 +.

16th Row.—P 8, Tf, P 2 +, P 1, Tf, P 2 +, P 1, Tf, P 1, P 2 +, P 2 +, Tf, P 1, Tf, P 1, P 2 +, Tf, P 1, P 2 +, Tf, P 9.

17th Row.—K 1, K 2 +, K 7, Tf, K 2, Tf, K 1, Tf, K 2 +, K 1, Tf, K 2 +, K 2 +, Tf, K 1, K 2 +, Tf, K 1, Tf, K 2, Tf, K 7, K 2 +.

18th Row.—P 2 +, P 7, Tf, P 2, Tf, P 3, Tf, P 2 +, P 1, Tf, P 2, Tf, P 1, P 2 +, Tf, P 3, Tf, P 2, Tf, P 7, P 2 +, P 1.

19th Row.—K 1, K 2 +, K 6, Tf, K 2, K 2 +, Tf, K 2, K 2 +, K 1, Tf, K 2, Tf, K 1, K 2 +, Tf, K 1, K 2 +, K 2, Tf, K 2 +, K 1, Tf, K 6, K 2 +.

20th Row.—P 2 +, P 5, Tf, P 1, P 2 +, Tf, P 2, P 2 +, P 2, Tf, P 2 +, P 1, Tf, P 2, Tf, P 1, P 2 +, Tf, P 2, P 2 +, P 2, Tf, P 2 +, P 1, Tf, P 5, P 2 +, P 1.

21st Row.—K 1, K 2 +, K 5, Tf, K 2, Tf, K 3, K 2 +, K 2, Tf, K 2 +, K 1, Tf, K 2, Tf, K 1, K 2 +, Tf, K 2, K 2 +, K 3, Tf, K 2, Tf, K 5, K 2 +.

22nd Row—P 2 +, P 4, Tf, P 1, P 2 +, Tf, P 8, Tf, P 2 +, P 1, Tf, P 2, Tf, P 1, P 2 +, Tf, P 8, Tf, P 2 +, P 1, Tf, P 4, P 2 +, P 1.

23rd Row.—K 1, K 2 +, K 4, Tf, K 3 +, K 3, K 2 +, K 4, Tf, K 2 +, K 1, Tf, K 2, Tf, K 1, K 2 +, Tf, K 4, K 2 +, K 3, K 3 +, Tf, K 4, K 2 +.

Figure 77. Sample of instructions.

Figure 79. Illustration accompanying pattern.

Knitters in continental Europe appear to have led the way in using charts for knitting lace. Perhaps this has been due to a need to overcome the problems arising from so many different languages in a relatively small area. Knitters elsewhere seem to have been slow to adopt the use of charts for knitting patterns, other than for Fair Isle and Intarsia style knitting. Probably the main incentive to use charts for lace has been the desire to obtain access to patterns from Europe. As proficiency has been learned, the added bonus of being able to use this skill to correct or adapt written instructions has been recognised.

There seem to be as many sets of chart symbols for recording lace in Europe as there are countries, and I gave up trying to track them all down. I have endeavoured to provide a reasonably representative selection in Appendix A, with some general comments. As well as these examples, I have included the better-known versions from English speaking countries.

The most complex example from Europe is the one from the magazine, *Burda*, published by Verlag Aenne Burda GmbH & Co. Offenburg, West Germany.

The symbols used for this system are very precise and reflect the extraordinary talent of their most memorable designer, Herbert Neibling. His work is not usually in the form of repetitive patterns, but each piece is designed as a whole and artistically translated into lace. There are designs for large pieces like table cloths and curtains, as well as small mats and edgings for doilies. The example in Figure 80 was knitted by Larry Smit of Madison, Wisconsin, in the United States of America.

The instructions for Neibling's pieces are in chart form, with

Figure 80. Edging designed by Neibling. Knitted by Larry Smit, Wisconsin, USA.

notes added only if there are any special directions. However, the symbols are introduced to the reader with written instructions describing each technique. Editions of this magazine with translations for those unable to read German are also available.

One of the truly impressive aspects of Neibling's designs is that he could, without the need to resort to yarn and needles to assist him in any way, make a chart of a totally new design.

In Britain, Marianne Kinzel, a wartime refugee from Europe, published in 1953 *A First Book of Modern Lace Knitting*, using charts as well as full written instructions. There have since been further editions of this very popular book, as well as of her second book, *Second Book of Modern Lace Knitting*, first published in 1961, which, in response to requests from her readers, shows the development of her designs to include complex interpretations of British floral emblems. Both books include written instructions as well as the charts, however the symbols for the latter are accompanied only by verbal descriptions in German and French, as well as English, and no illustrations of the techniques. These symbols are included in Appendix A.

One of the most popular series of books in the United States are the three treasuries of knitting patterns written by Barbara G. Walker of New Jersey. However, it is not until *Charted Knitting Designs*, her third treasury, that she introduces the reader to the use of charts for lace. With minor alterations, her system is the one I now use as I find the symbols quick and easy to draw on a chart and they usually relate visually to the technique they represent. Appendix A.

As with any system it is the user who will decide which system serves them the best and preferences will no doubt be based on a variety of reasons. There have been times when it has been a better solution for me to translate a chart from a strange or confusing system of symbols to one with which I am familiar in order to enjoy the project.

During the exercises in the following chapters, reference will be made to various methods of recording and their suitability. As the knitter works through these, and reaches the stage of recording new and original patterns, the need will arise for a choice to be made as to a method of recording the data which is both easy to use and to understand.

5. Planning Projects

୫

*Using tension measurements, charts
and construction techniques.*

To make the best possible use of the samples and information
from the preceding chapters, from further exploration and from
personal experience already gained, it is necessary to have a
system whereby this information is always readily accessible and
can be added to easily.

Whatever method is chosen some thought needs to be given
to durability. Folders with plastic pockets can be very useful for
this purpose, as the order of the contents can be easily
reorganized and it can be an advantage to remove material
required for a specific project to a 'working folder' for the period
needed and then, subsequently, to return it to the main file.
However, do not be tempted to overload a folder beyond its
capacity, as paper in particular is very heavy and can place a
great deal of stress on the container.

To be of use, resource material has to be easy to find and to
refer to, and should be accompanied by relevant notes as it is
surprising how quickly that information which, at the time it is
received seems very obvious, may become a mystery several years
later! Details of needle size and yarn used for samples,
accompanied by construction details and comments, are most
important.

It is sometimes very helpful to repeat the same information
in more than one place—especially if it is likely to be frequently
used in more than one context—and it saves time in cross
referencing; for example, Fisherman's Rib may be in two
sections—'value scale' and 'lace backgrounds'. Remember also
to include a section of working drawings, calculations and a
photograph of the finished project so as to remind you of what
you have accomplished and to act, not only as a record, but as
future inspiration for further variations, or completely new ideas.

A most valuable resource is at least one dictionary of knitting
patterns, ranging from traditional to modern variations and
new designs. With the revival of interest in knitting, there are

Figure 81. File for resource material.

Figure 82. File for specific project.

many of these currently available, some with written instructions and others with charts. Others have both versions.

Magazines, pattern brochures and leaflets are also valuable resource references for new designs and patterns. However, sort through such collections frequently, and be selective as it is very easy to simply become a 'collector' or 'hoarder' and rarely use much of the material acquired.

From time to time you will see illustrations, maybe from nature photography, reproductions of paintings, or sometimes even a 'scribble', that may seem to have possibilities for an original design or an 'interpretation' in lace knitting. It is worthwhile to keep these in a separate folder, so they can be referred to when searching for ideas relating to a new project. Figure 81.

As you find patterns which you feel relate to any of these ideas, this information can also be added. Such reminders may be in the form of a reference to another file, or to a book of your own, or a library book. These patterns could be anything from background possibilities to more complex patterns which suggest similar shapes or effects which could provide ideas for constructing a design you wish to develop.

If you see a really definite possibility which you would like to follow through, start a separate file and add to it samples and information which could be of specific use when developing that project. This could include knitted samples of patterns from a knitting dictionary which resemble, or contain features which may be utilized in some way, yarn samples and colour samples—and possible construction details ready for being put together as the idea takes shape. Figure 82.

Sometimes the idea comes together very quickly, but usually it needs time to 'germinate' and for one's subconscious to 'process' it first. The quest for new ideas can sometimes result in many months of searching and trying out different yarns and stitches before a solution can be reached; however, during this period, there is often the bonus of new discoveries to be filed away, to be developed at a later time, as can be seen in Figure 83.

When the time comes for calculations to be made to enable the execution of a project, it is necessary to construct a series of tension squares from which a choice can be made as to the appropriate needle size and grist of yarn to be used and, with this decision made, the number of stitches and rows for a given measurement can be ascertained.

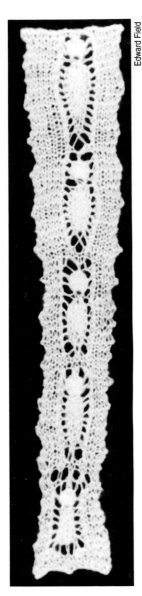

Edward Field

Figure 83. Kowhai flower and Kakabeak flower development.

Figure 84. Tension squares with several patterns.

It is recommended that at least three variations of needle size be made for the chosen yarn, and that the tension square be of a size that will accommodate all the stitch variations which will be used in the finished article. This latter exercise is essential to see how the different patterns work in relation to each other, as demonstrated in Figure 84.

To complete the tension square once it has been constructed, it needs to be washed and finished in the same way as the completed article is to be finished—for example, blocked under tension, or eased into shape.

The need to carry out this stage was demonstrated to me when I was commissioned in 1982, by the High Country Sheep Breeders of the South Island of New Zealand, to design, spin and knit a shawl for the Prince and Princess of Wales to celebrate the birth of Prince William. As my time was very limited I decided, as a trial-run for needle-size, patterns and measurements, to spin and knit a Christening coat for my first grandchild, due the month before the Royal baby. It is just as well I did, for although I had worked out all the individual motifs and the insertion pattern to give the measurements I required, when they were assembled together as a garment, the fabric of the insertion pattern had the appearance of having been knitted on larger needles than the rest of the garment as can be seen in Figure 85. This was not such a problem when used as the border

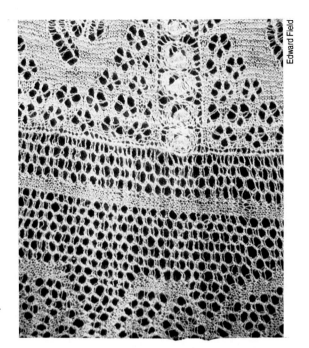

Edward Field

Figure 85. Detail of christening coat.

Michael Mihajlovic

Figure 86. Shawl.

of the coat, but it was not acceptable for a flat piece like a shawl. The shawl was, therefore, knitted with size 2mm needles, except for the insertion which was knitted on size 1.5mm needles. As can be seen in Figure 86, this meant that the values used to express the total design of the shawl were balanced and consistent.

Completed tension squares will provide the following information:

1) The effect that needle size, yarn and tension used has on the fabric.
2) Lace-pattern definition in relation to needle size, yarn and tension used.
3) How many stitches are required for a given width, using a specified needle size, yarn and tension.
4) How many rows are required for a given length, using a specified needle size, yarn and tension.

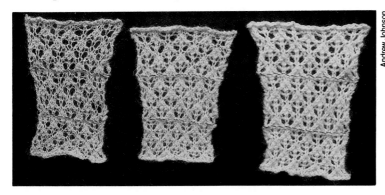

Andrew Johnson

Figure 87. Information from tension squares - different yarns and needles for same patterns.

Some examples demonstrating the use of the information provided by the tension squares in Figure 87, and using the criteria as stated above, would be as follows:

1) A final decision as to whether or not the appearance, flexibility, density and handle of the fabric is appropriate to the planned project.

If there is dissatisfaction about any of these criteria, then further experiments need to be made to find a better solution. For example

Appearance: consider the texture, colour, lustre and similar aspects. Is this the overall effect required?

Flexibility: consider the choice of materials and the amount of twist. Is this affected by patterns, materials, or a combination of both? If it is designed to drape, will it do so?

Density: consider needle-size in relation to the grist of the yarn. The extremes being the fabric is too solid or too loose. Decide by considering the appearance of the overall fabric. **Handle:** does it feel good and does it feel appropriate for its end use? Is the yarn too hard, too scratchy or too soft, too thick or too filmy?

Once there is satisfaction about the above qualities it is time to consider the next stage.

2) Patterns need to work in harmony.

The decisions to be made from the information gathered here is how the patterns look in relation to each other. Are they of uniform density so as to balance each other? Do the solid areas provide sufficient contrast to the open areas to give definition to the design? Check density, as above.

Perhaps the patterns are a mixture of lace knitting and knitted lace and adjustments need to be made, or alternatives tried, to ensure an overall harmony as illustrated in Figures 88 and 89.

Check your value scale again. There may be a better choice of stitch for you to use which gives the same value as the one which may be giving a problem. Maybe some new samples from a knitting treasury hold the solution.

This is now the time to make decisions about how the patterns will be positioned, as it may be possible to design the construction of the article to accommodate an especially favoured pattern. Perhaps different sized needles from those being used for other parts of the project are required and it could be that 'short rows' may be necessary for the pattern to work.

Knitting part of the article from a different direction may be the answer to overcoming a problem encountered by the decision to choose a pattern for a particular position in the design.

When a pleasing solution has been reached then the final decisions on the size, shape and construction of the article can be made. By using the information provided in Figure 89, an example of how to use the information described in 3 above, see tension squares, would be as follows: to make an article from pattern A measuring 10 centimetres (4 inches) wide, cast on 28 stitches, as 7 stitches measure 2.5 centimetres (1 inch). 12.5 centimetres (5 inches) would require 35 stitches.

Having worked out the width then the information described in 4 above can be used to calculate the number of rows required as follows: for a length of 25 centimetres (10 inches), 120 rows

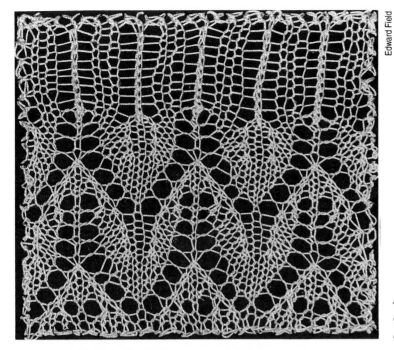

Figure 88. Inappropriate combination of knitted lace and lace knitting.

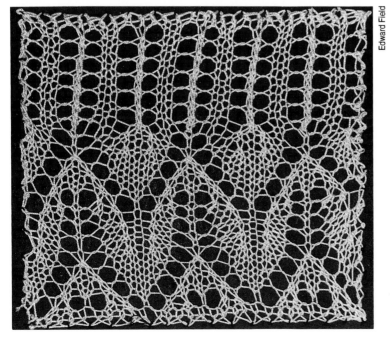

Figure 89. Harmonious combination of knitted lace and lace knitting.

need to be worked, as 12 rows are required for 2.5 centimetres (1 inch). 24 rows would give 5 centimetres (2 inches).

When there are several patterns involved, as in Figure 89, then separate calculations may need to be made for each pattern. As discussed earlier, in Chapter 3, the way the holes are made and the open nature of the pattern can vary the width and length of the piece considerably, and it may be necessary to accommodate this by changing the number of stitches for working that particular section of the design. Sometimes this can be very convenient in that by moving from a pattern using a 'make one' construction, to a pattern using a 'yarn over' construction—at a point where the shape requires an increase in width—then this can be done without increasing the number of stitches. See Figure 90. This is also a technique used for some circular pieces, in that the shaped centre is worked in a stocking stitch or garter stitch and then the first part of the border is worked in an open pattern, so allowing the total area to lie flat when it has been washed and blocked. The edging on these shawls is invariably worked sideways, picking up one stitch from the centre for each two rows of the border. This gives the extra fullness needed to keep the circle flat. Figure 91.

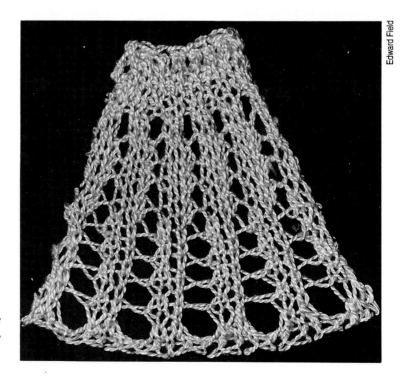

Edward Field

Figure 90. Shaping a yoke using 'yarn over' and 'make one' techniques.

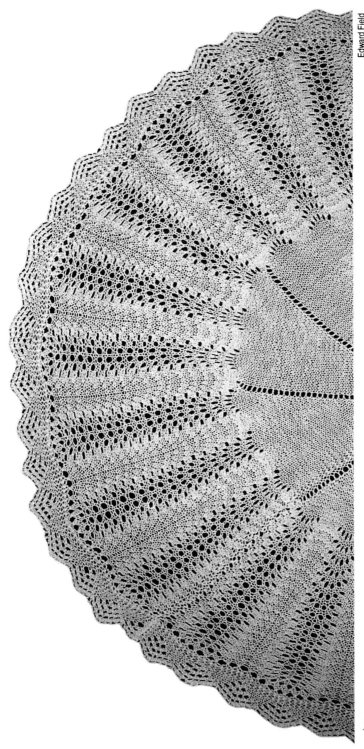

Edward Field

Figure 91. 'Bubbles' shawl.

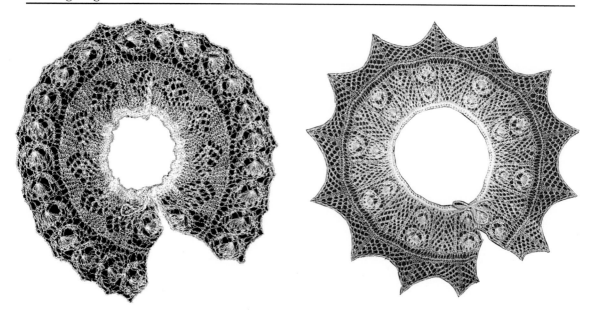

Figure 92. Collar.

Figure 93. Collar.

Collars are small projects which can give practice in using some of the construction techniques which have been described.

For the first two collars, begin by making a small tension square in stocking stitch using the yarn and needles chosen. Wash, block and record measurements.

The first one, Figure 92, is a simple construction using double stocking stitch to shape the neck band. It is knitted sideways throughout and a graft at the centre back is needed only if the pattern has a 'top' and a 'bottom'. The tension square will tell the knitter how many rows need to be worked to give the length of neck edge required. For the first one it is a good idea to choose an edging pattern which looks the same from either direction. Add 16 to 20 stitches to the straight edge of the pattern and knit these in double stocking stitch. This edge will make a firm casing for the collar to be either attached by sewing, or through which a cord may be threaded. At the same time, the edge is drawn in to shape the collar as the depth in rows is half that of the rest of the knitting. This means that double the number of rows need to be worked overall for the length required.

The second collar illustrates how changes in direction can be used to effect the shaping. Figure 93.

Start by choosing a simple, symmetrical edge stitch for the outer border. When this has been knitted to the required length, cast off. Pick up and knit one stitch for every two rows along the straight edge and work a further pattern to complement the pattern used for the edging. Finish the collar by working 16 to 20 rows of double stocking stitch without changing the number of stitches. To decide the number of stitches, refer to the tension square and decide how many stitches are required to give the width to fit around the neck edge. Double this number which will then be the number of stitches to be picked up along the border. Double this number again to find out the number of rows for the border.

The third collar is a straight flat strip but using different directions. It is gathered into a frill with a twisted cord. Figure 94.

It will be necessary to make a tension square in the lace patterns chosen, to estimate the number of rows required for the outer edge and the measurement of the depth of the collar, which will be the depth of the edging plus the number of rows required to complete the insertion pattern.

Proceed as for the second collar until the stitches along the border have been picked up—one stitch for each two rows. On the next row increase in every third stitch. With few exceptions, this formula works to keep the fabric flat. Continue with the chosen insertion pattern and then, to work the edging along the top edge, work one row of eyelets followed by a second row, knitting every third and fourth stitch together.

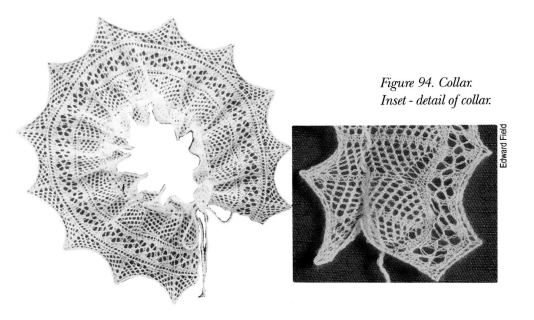

Figure 94. Collar.
Inset - detail of collar.

Edward Field

Knit the edging by casting on the base number of stitches and then knit the last stitch of the straight edge, together with a stitch from the insertion on every alternate row until all the stitches have been worked off. If the edging pattern has a row of eyelets along the straight edge, then the eyelet row worked before the decrease row can be eliminated.

Make small segments illustrating these techniques and include them with the instructions and any of your own comments in your file.

One of the most noticeable conclusions to be reached when making a tension square is that rarely, if ever, does the number of stitches and rows to a given measurement work out to be the same. Almost without exception, the number of rows to be worked to make a square is greater than the number of stitches. Consequently, regular graph paper can be used for recording patterns, but it does not provide us with an accurate shape, or measurement, of the article being designed.

This does not need to be a problem and since I have discovered, in most of my workshops on designing original lace, that many people seem to be nervous when it comes to using charts, the following exercises may be of help. Even if charts seem to be intimidating to begin with, by moving slowly from one stage to the other the reward will be well worthwhile as they provide such freedom and control when it comes to designing accurate shapes.

Exercise 1

You will need a pattern for a garment of back, front and sleeves to fit a baby or small child. Preferably one you have used before. Additionally, you will need regular graph paper, pencil and ruler.

Using the instructions from the pattern, draw on the graph paper a chart of the shape of all pieces of the garment. Each square represents one stitch.

This is done by ruling a line under the number of stitches for the cast-on edge. For example: Cast on 60 sts would mean ruling a line under 60 squares. Knit 10 rows in k1, p1, rib, would mean drawing a line along 10 squares at right angles to the line already drawn. Figure 95.

Figure 96 shows how increasing in every 10th stitch would be shown, followed by 30 rows of plain knitting.

Figure 97 shows how the armholes would be portrayed if the instructions given were for 3 sts to be cast off at the beginning of the next 2 rows, followed by a decrease at the armhole edge every alternate row, until 26 sts remain.

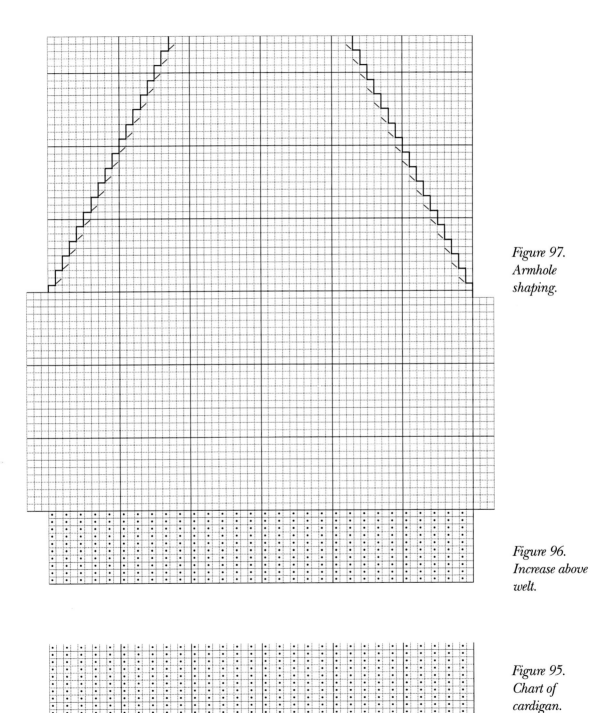

*Figure 97.
Armhole
shaping.*

*Figure 96.
Increase above
welt.*

*Figure 95.
Chart of
cardigan.*

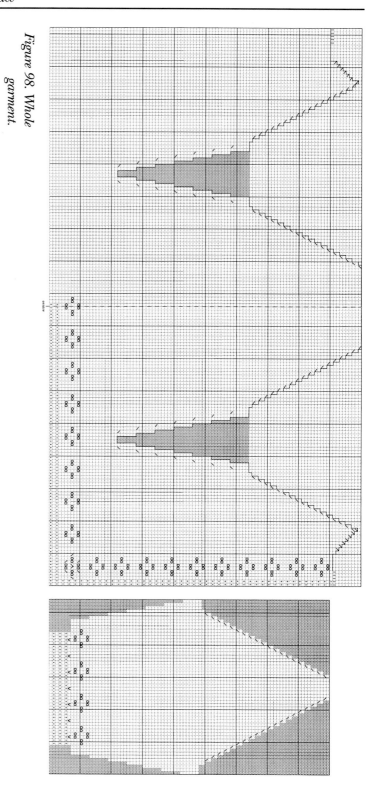

Figure 98. Whole garment.

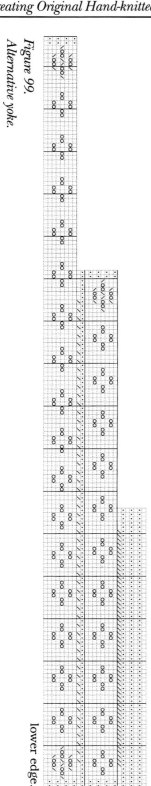

Figure 99. Alternative yoke.

lower edge.

Figure 98 shows a chart of a whole garment done this way.

In Figure 99, a solution is shown for making a chart of a circular yoke. For any design where there are major changes in stitch numbers on one row, this is usually the easiest way to represent the new shape and to make a workable chart for organizing pattern placement.

Each square represents one stitch so, although the chart is going to appear to be more squat than the actual garment, if the tension square you have made matches the one given at the beginning of the pattern instructions, it will be possible to knit this pattern to fit the size for which it was designed.

Now that you have a 'picture' of the garment it is possible for you to make it your own 'original'.

You could choose a lace insertion pattern to place above the rib. If the multiple of stitches you need to use is too few, or too many, to fit on the number of stitches available, you will be able to place the extra stitches (or delete stitches) so as not to upset the shape of the garment. It could be a better solution to combine the stitches for the fronts and the back and place the insertion pattern across all the stitches, using the chart to centre the pattern.

At this point it is unnecessary to record all the symbols of the pattern. Either pencil the 'yarn over' symbol in the squares where these occur to give you a visual effect of the placement of the pattern, or simply outline the set of squares which represent each pattern repeat. Colour pencils can often be helpful at this stage of the planning. Figure 98.

Where adjustments need to be made to suit the pattern, it is much easier to follow through these changes when the garment can be seen with each stitch accounted for, as then other parts of the garment can be also adjusted before knitting starts. An example of this is where stitches are added or subtracted and this changes the armhole shaping. With the sleeve also in chart form complementary changes can be made to ensure a successful fit.

Still using regular graph paper it is also possible successfully to chart simple shapes by using a tension square and having definite dimensions.

The tension square tells the number of stitches and rows to give 5cms (2 inches). Therefore, the number of stitches to give the width of the article can be calculated. If the width changes at intervals, then the tension square will also provide information on how many stitches are required for these new measurements and, at the same time, the number of rows between these changes in stitch numbers can also be calculated. This allows a chart to be drawn, and it is then a case of deciding on the method of changing these stitch numbers in the number of rows available in order to achieve the shape required and also to ensure that it is in harmony with the pattern being used in the design. Figure 100.

One of the advantages of using the graph paper, as described above, is that the size of the squares can be enlarged to a size which is easy to see and this can be a big advantage for very fine, knitted lace where there is pattern information on every row with a variety of symbols.

Figure 100. Christening coat.

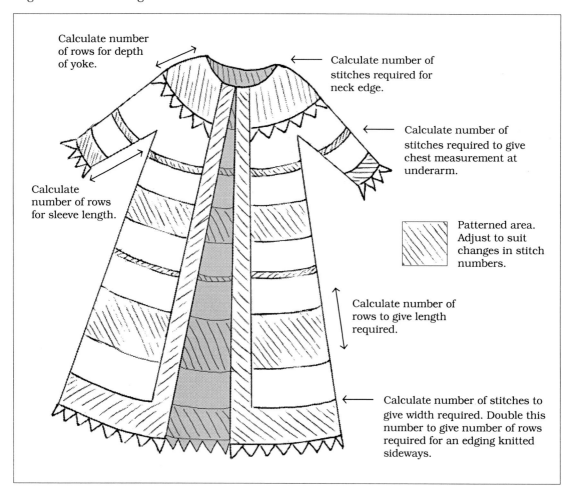

Calculate number of rows for depth of yoke.

Calculate number of stitches required for neck edge.

Calculate number of stitches required to give chest measurement at underarm.

Calculate number of rows for sleeve length.

Patterned area. Adjust to suit changes in stitch numbers.

Calculate number of rows to give length required.

Calculate number of stitches to give width required. Double this number to give number of rows required for an edging knitted sideways.

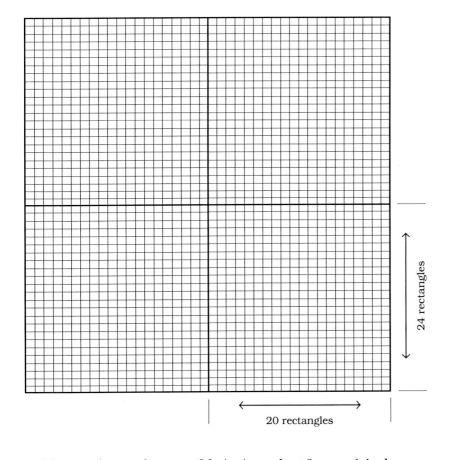

24 rectangles

20 rectangles

Figure 101.
'Knitters graph'

There is also another way of designing a chart for an original shape. This is to use 'knitter's graph' paper. It can be bought in a variety of tension readings or, alternatively, it is not difficult to make it yourself. This graph paper is drawn to represent the actual size of the stitches. For example, to make a 'knitter's graph' to show 20 stitches and 24 rows to measure 5cms (2 inches), a square measuring 5cms would be divided into 20 across the bottom and top and 24 along each side and ruled to make a square of 20 rectangles by 24 rectangles. Figure 101. Using a photocopier, to reproduce enough to join with clear tape to make a page, then gives you a 'master copy' from which you can make as many sheets as you wish, and which you can join to make even larger sheets.

Figure 102. Shaped edge.

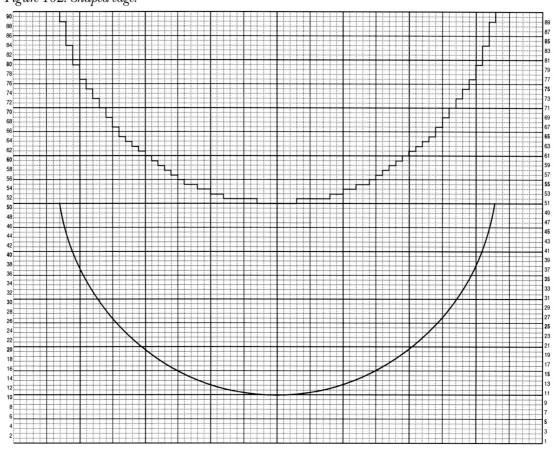

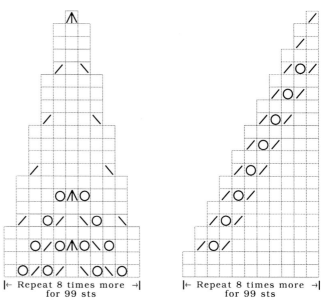

Figure 103. Back of bonnet.

|← Repeat 8 times more →|
for 99 sts

|← Repeat 8 times more →|
for 99 sts

To use 'knitter's graph' paper simply place a template of the shape you wish to knit on the graph and trace around it. Remove the shape and then 'fine tune' the outline to plot the position of increases, decreases etc. Using a dressmaking pattern for knit fabrics is a good practice for this method. Figure 102.

If there are concave shapes, then work out suitable places where cuts can be made in the template, just as darts are used in a dressmaker's pattern to allow it to lie flat and where the knitted shaping will work in harmony with the overall design. Typical solutions for knitting these shapes would include using 'short rows' and decreasing or increasing on one or both sides of a segment. Figure 103 shows the solution for the crown of a hat. Other examples could be heel and instep shaping, circular yokes, collars and sleeves.

The big advantage of this type of graph paper is that it is a representation of the actual dimensions of the article, as well as of all the stitches. Additionally, once the article is drawn up—and shape problems have been solved—the chart, for ease of use can be enlarged and reference, if and when necessary, made to the actual dimensions on the original chart.

There are times when all the information which comes up during a planning exercise is not necessary for the project in hand. For example, the extra tension squares made when experimenting with different yarns, needle sizes, patterns etc. However, once all this information has been worked out it should be recorded, even if you do not plan to use all of it on the current project. There is always the possibility it could save time and effort in the future, as well as being a possible source of further inspiration.

6. Being in Control

Manipulating lace to suit your requirements

The next step along the journey is to learn to feel confident with the structure of traditional lace patterns. By understanding how they work, it is then possible to use and adapt these patterns to suit a new design. It also gives practice in reaching solutions for expressing new ideas.

Most knitters of lace have worked simple diamond shapes, and the first of this next series of exercises should, therefore, not be too daunting.

Figure 104 shows a chart with 'yarn over' symbols. As each 'yarn over' is introducing a new stitch, then for each 'yarn over' a stitch must be removed to keep the number of stitches constant.

Make three copies of this chart. In the first chart, enter decrease symbols where you think they should be to give a solution which will give the diamond shape shown and knit your solution in stocking stitch.

If you placed the decreases next to the 'yarn over' symbols, did they create a chain effect as shown in the diamond at the top of Figure 105? If not can you change the decrease symbols

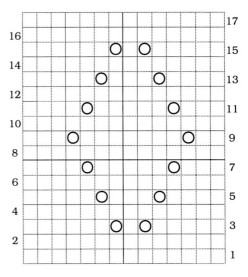

Figure 104. Diamond shape.

Edward Field

Figure 105. Diamond with chain effect.

to achieve this? Use the second chart to record this change and knit another sample to illustrate this.

If you did achieve the chain effect the first time, then use your second chart to change the decreases to eliminate the chain and knit a sample to illustrate this.

Use your third chart to keep the stitch numbers correct, but locate the decreases as far from the 'yarn overs' as possible and knit your solution.

Perhaps you were unable to keep the shape of the diamond intact? If this was the case then study Figure 106.

The most important principle to learn from these exercises, and one which because it is often taken for granted when working such a simple shape, is that, as the solid area becomes smaller the decreases must be located in this area. Conversely, the method for increasing is located in the area where the solid area becomes larger. For a designer this can at times be a most inconvenient fact, however, one that must be acknowledged and there are manipulations, when necessary, which can be employed to place increases and decreases in positions which do not detract from a design.

Figure 106. Three diamond solutions.

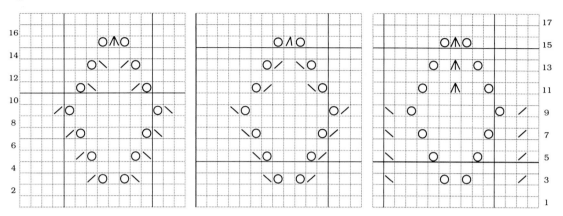

This exercise should also illustrate the reason why the bias occurs in Figure 48 (see Chapter 3, page 41) and how this can be used so effectively to make the edging. The first and third diamonds in Figure 106 show the two solutions most commonly used and you will recognise them as the basis for many traditional lace patterns. Making a feature of the decreases, or not, is a decision for the designer. The most significant difference with the third example, other than the 'yarn overs' being located in the fabric on their own, is that the cast-on and cast-off edges are shaped by the build-up of decreases in one section of the fabric. This is a principle often used to give pointed and scalloped edgings in lace that is knitted. A well-known example of a pattern commonly used which uses this technique with great effect is 'Old Shale' or 'Feather and Fan'.

One of the problems less easy to solve is to knit this diamond with the chain as a design feature which outlines the holes of the diamond, as shown at the bottom of Figure 105.

If you enjoy a challenge make another copy of Figure 104 and try and reach a solution. The principles involved here will be covered later in this Chapter on page 99.

By now it should be possible for the reader to make a chart of simple lace patterns from the material already covered in the preceding chapters and, with the help of the systems in Appendix A, more complex charts can be attempted.

As an exercise to test this knowledge, make charts for several lace patterns from a knitting treasury, starting with one you have knitted before and feel you know well. Knit it at the same time, so that you relate not only the words with the symbols, but also the action of the technique.

Figures 107, 108, 109 and 110 show examples of knitted lace, lace knitting, creative lace and a pattern where the number of stitches in a row varies. The charts have been made to indicate the appearance of the pattern.

See if you can give the written instructions for these patterns. They can all be found in Barbara G. Walker's *Second Treasury of Knitting Patterns*, as well as in many other treasuries.

With a coloured pencil, colour each increase (which may be a 'make one', a 'yarn over' etc.) with its matching decrease, in copies of the charts in Figures 107—110. Notice how they contribute to the overall design.

Figure 107. Coral pattern.

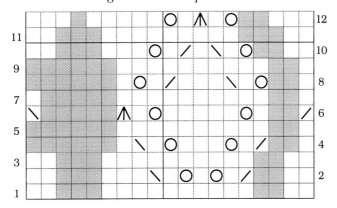

Figure 108. Milanese Lace.

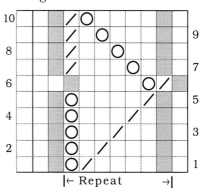

Figure 109. Lotus pattern.

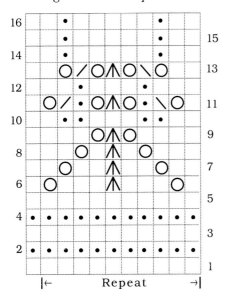

Figure 110. Wineglass lace.

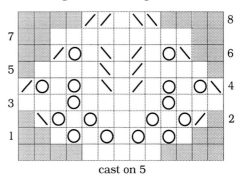

Figure 111. Sleeve shaping.

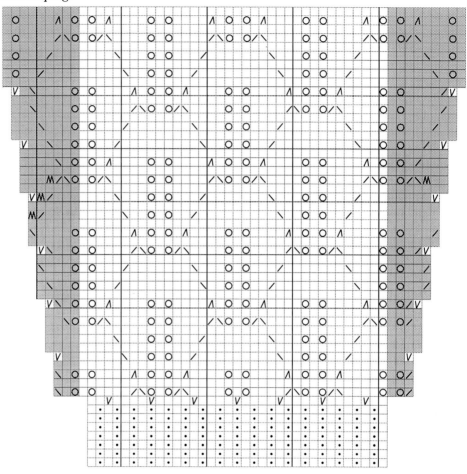

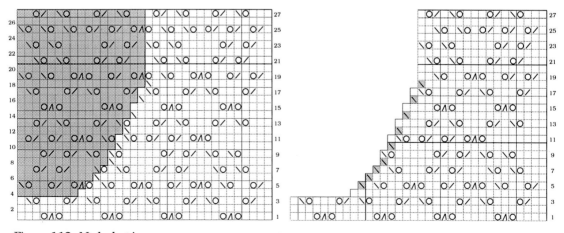

Figure 112. Neck shaping.

This ability to analyse the way a pattern works is very useful, even when knitting a pattern which gives you all the instructions EXCEPT, for example, how to deal with those extra stitches which build up when increasing along the edge of a sleeve in an all over lace-pattern garment. Or how to deal with keeping the pattern correct when shaping the neck edge!

The answer is to make a chart of one repeat of the pattern on the centre of a sheet of graph paper. Work out the number of rows the shaping will cover and chart just this section either side of the pattern, Figures 111 and 112. Now fill in the pattern over the new stitches, overlapping the shaping line where necessary. Then, with coloured pencils, colour in the matching increases and decreases of the pattern as in the exercise above. Now check where the shaping line is situated in relation to the components which form the pattern, as it may happen that the extra stitch required for an increase can be achieved by leaving out a pattern decrease. For example, where an increase is required, if the last two stitches of a pattern were to be 'yo, k2 tog' then 'yo, k2' could solve the problem.

The solution is not always as easy as this example, but having the requirements for keeping the pattern correctly set out visually, it is much easier to improvise and keep track of the number of stitches involved, as well as being able to decide which elements of the design it is best to keep intact and which can be sacrificed to allow for shaping.

When designing shapes where the knitter wants to use part of a pattern to make an edging, or perhaps to fit a corner, charts can again play a useful part.

Using the diamond motif again, make two charts for edgings. The first one using the whole diamond shape and the second, a narrower one which uses half the diamond. Figure 113.

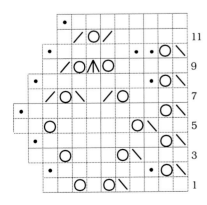
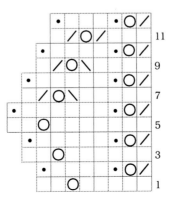

Figure 113. Edging from diamond.

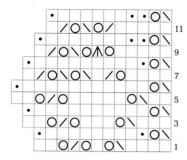

Using colour pencils to shade in the areas which are to be deleted make it clearer; then pair the 'yarn overs' with the corresponding decreases. Decide which decreases are to be eliminated to make the zigzag effect. Using a different colour, add any extra stitches which are required to complete the pattern. In this case, an extra stitch along the shaped edge. Another solution is where the zigzag effect is accentuated by an extra row of holes as shown in Figure 114.

Try another pattern, like a leaf pattern, following the above procedure. As long as your solution works and pleases you there is no 'right answer' as you are now the designer!

A mitred corner is an effective way of dealing with square or triangular shapes which have a border or corner shaping, and the system described for edgings can be used for this chart also.

Make as many repeats of the pattern as required for the completion of the corner, and colour the unwanted area. The more the pattern is based on diamond, square or other symmetrical shapes the easier it is to work out a harmonious solution. However, when this is not the case, it is necessary to look carefully to see which shapes are those making the most impact in the design and work on a result which keeps this

Figure 114. Embellished diamond edge.

Figure 115. Corner on horizontal border.

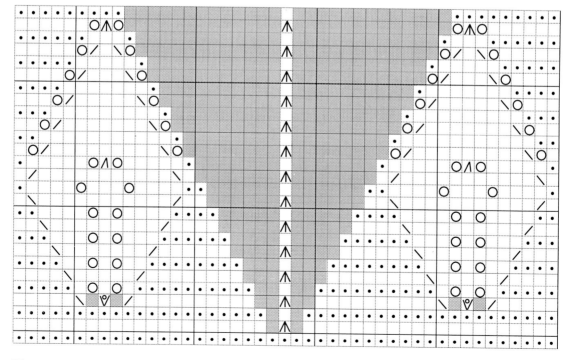

90

effect intact. This is a time when several ideas may need to be tried before a satisfactory result is obtained.

The shaping itself may need to be done on a horizontal version, as in Figure 115, or on a vertical border as in Figure 116.

In the horizontal version there may be a choice of how the decreasing is done to accommodate the pattern. In the vertical version, the system of working 'short rows' can be used. It will be necessary to employ some method to avoid a hole forming where the work is turned.

The most popular and effective method, in my experience, is to slip the first of the stitches to be left with the yarn in front. Take yarn to back then slip stitch back on to left-hand needle, thus making a loop around the slipped stitch. When this stitch is later knitted, the loop is knitted with the stitch that was slipped. This method is usually referred to as 'wrapping', Figure 117.

A 'wrapped' stitch is not shown as an extra stitch on the chart, but can be indicated with a different colour if desired. Check your resource file for other methods you may have collected, and try any other alternatives you may see in other publications and record these with your own evaluation for future reference.

Dropped stitches in lace that is knitted can be described only as a nightmare! Making a chart of a pattern can sometimes come to the rescue in such a

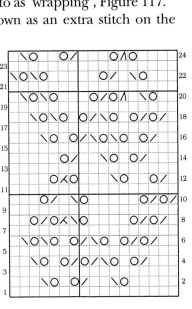

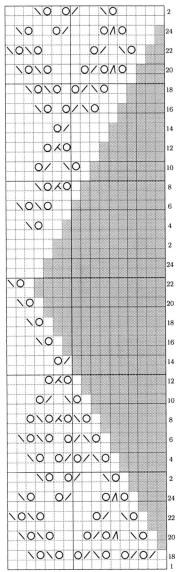

Figure 116. Corner on vertical border.

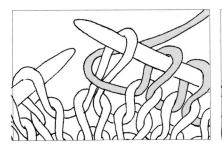

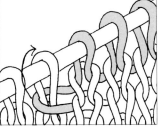

Figure 117. Wrapped stitch.

91

case or, when a repair needs to be made. Unfortunately, much depends on the complexity and construction of individual patterns and often the best answer in the end, if the tension is to remain consistent and the fibre is not to be weakened, is to 'capture the runaway stitches' with a safety pin and then 'unknit', stitch by stitch, back to where they can be returned to their place in the fabric.

To 'unknit' it's a lot easier if needles at least two sizes smaller are used, and then return to the correct size as soon as the knitting recommences.

It is worthwhile to stage a 'rescue' if it seems at all possible and the chart in this case is used to identify the path of each lost stitch. Once again, use a coloured pencil to colour the path of the lost stitch. This will show straight away any involvement with neighbouring stitches on its journey. Tapestry needles, to hold the stitches involved, together with the help of a crochet hook to ease the interlacing during the retrieval, make useful tools. Figure 118.

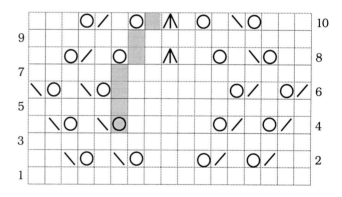

Figure 118. Dropped stitches.

This technique also works for a tear or pulled thread. When broken threads are involved, then new thread will need to be introduced and this will require to be matched carefully. Once the movement of the stitches has been arrested, place them on short, fine needles or tapestry needles. Bring in new thread, a separate length for each row, and re-knit each row once again using a crochet hook to assist. Use a grafting technique to reinforce the stitches surrounding the repair with the new thread left from each repair row. Figure 119. Sometimes a dense foam or polystyrene pad held behind the work can provide a very useful surface on which to pin stitches in place.

Repair work often presents the problem of having to deal

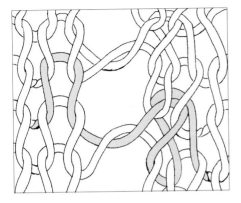

Figure 119. Repairing a hole.

with a stitch for which one does not have instructions! This is a challenge which should no longer be insurmountable, now that the exploration of lace is revealing so many secrets.

This problem can be approached as follows:

First question: is it knitted lace or lace knitting or a combination of both?

If it is knitted lace then there will be a pattern worked on every row. If it is lace knitting the pattern will be worked on every alternate row. Creative Lace ? Be ready for anything!

Second question: is it a garter stitch or stocking stitch background? Or a combination?

Third question: is it a repeating pattern? If this is so, then decide how many stitches make up one pattern repeat. Also how many rows. A magnifying glass may be needed to see this. Thread a needle with contrasting thread and run a thread along each side of one repeat.

Fourth question: is it easier to identify the position of the 'yarn overs' or the decreases? Whatever the answer to this, make a chart and place them where they appear to belong, then include as much other information as you can glean from the knitting.

Fifth question: does the chart work as it stands? If the 'yarn overs' and decreases are not balanced, for example, then improvise by using a different coloured pencil to make the adjustments you feel will correct this with a view to making any changes necessary as the solutions hopefully emerge when knitting a sample of the chart.

Sixth question: how does the knitted sample compare with the original? Use the magnifying glass to help identify any problems and if the techniques you have used to copy the original have not produced the effect you require—and you do not have any alternatives to try—then check a knitting treasury or list of techniques to see if you can identify a similar result in another pattern.

Knitting Lace by Susanna E. Lewis, published by The Taunton Press, U.S.A. is an excellent reference for those with a particular interest in this area.

There have been several occasions when I have been asked to complete a piece of knitting which has been inherited, unfinished and with the pattern missing. For sentimental reasons it has been important to the owner that, if at all possible, the knitting should be completed and it is very satisfying to be able to work out a pattern for this to be done.

As the reader's experience with charts grows, there are even more possibilities to explore. Adding and deleting parts of patterns to fit particular shapes, making borders and edgings, as well as devising corners and other improvisations, have been looked at. There are also other ways whereby patterns can be reorganised to suit the designer.

In 'Wild Flower Posy', Figure 120, which features in my book *Handspinning, Dyeing and Working with Merino and Superfine Wools* published by The Caxton Press, New Zealand, (and co-published by Robert Hale, London, Kangaroo Press, Sydney and Interweave Press, Colorado) is an example of using basic traditional patterns and making changes to them for use in a different context.

The border to this pattern is the Buttercup edging which is featured on page 376 in Barbara G. Walker's *A Second Treasury of Knitting Patterns*. This has been knitted according to the instructions given and a chart made. While the border was being knitted, note was taken of the stitches which formed the actual buttercup shape and the way in which the adjacent stitches related to the formation of the flower and this was recorded on the chart. Figure 121.

Edward Field

Figure 120. Wild Flower Posy.

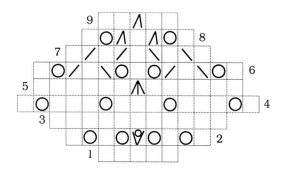

Figure 121. Buttercup.

It was also noted that the flower could be used to decrease the number of stitches and was eventually used as two repeats at the centre of the piece.

The next pattern to be introduced was the 'Snowdrop' or 'Bluebell' depending on the publication in which it appears. A version of this pattern is called 'Window Border' on page 347 of *A Second Treasury of Knitting Patterns*.

The pattern was knitted first as given in traditional texts and then a variation widening the division between each flower shape was used. The traditional version was later used to reduce the number of stitches in each multiple and to place more emphasis on the flower shape. Figure 122. This pattern has been adapted even further as shown in Figure 123 and is featured in the 'Bluebell Baby Set' in Appendix B.

The third pattern to be used was a daisy-shape with six petals. This pattern was changed by adding a 'bobble' for the centre of the daisy to give both texture and more definition to the flower. Figure 124.

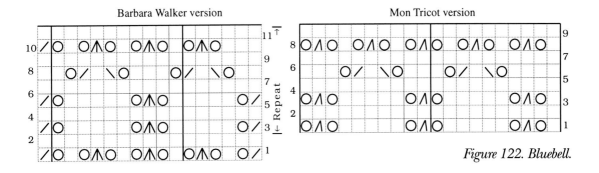

Figure 122. Bluebell.

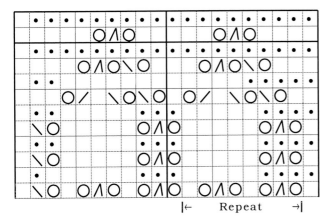

|← Repeat →|

Figure 123. Redesigned bluebell.

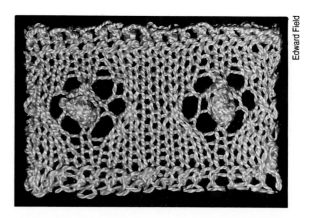

Edward Field

Figure 124. Daisy with bobble centre.

Select several patterns from a knitting treasury, make a chart of each one, of two or three repeats, depending on the complexity of the pattern, and practise isolating an element from each pattern. Test your success by knitting the results and 'fine tune' to reach a pleasing solution. Figure 125 gives an example.

Earlier, in Chapter 5, knitting in different directions, when constructing an article was discussed. To do this complications can arise where a pattern, which works well knitted in one direction, does not work well if the direction is changed. For example, totally symmetrical shapes like a square or a diamond

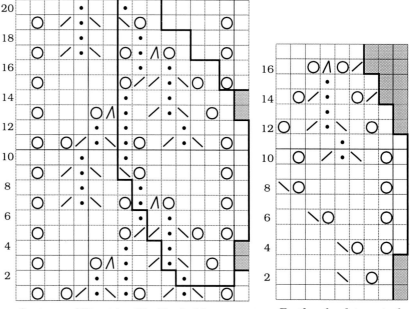

Figure 125. Leaf from repeating pattern.

Source of written instructions 'Barbara Walker's A Treasury of Knitting Patterns' p 217.

2 repeats of 'Drooping Elm' leaf with one leaf outlined.

Further development of leaf shape.

rarely cause problems, especially if the decrease does not form a feature in the design as in Figure 126.

An example when it can be useful to change the direction of a pattern, is when the design in a horizontal border is required for a matching edging, knitted from the other direction.

To illustrate this I have chosen 'Versailles Border' from Barbara G. Walker's *A Second Treasury of Knitting Patterns*, page 348.

Figure 126. Diamonds in different directions.

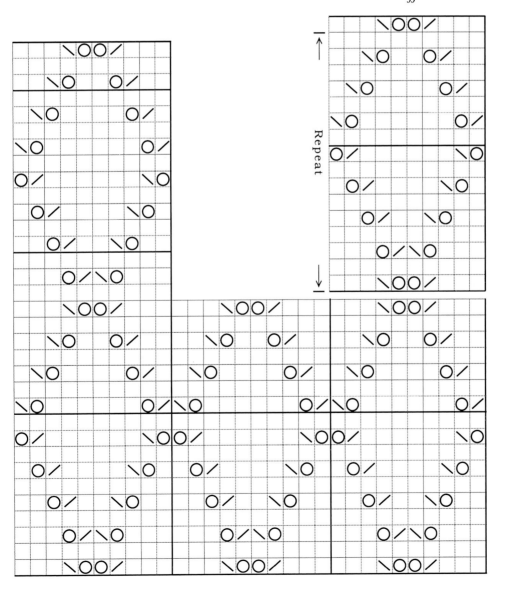

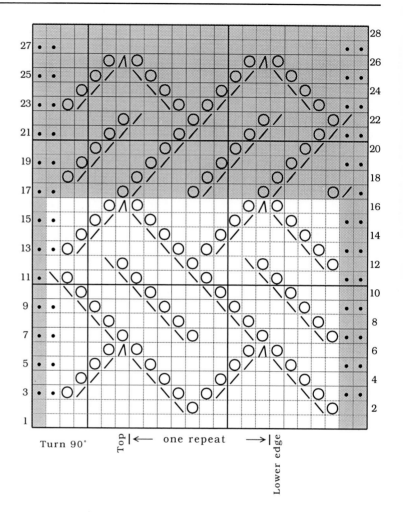

Figure 127. Versailles border.

Turn 90° — Top |← one repeat →| Lower edge

First of all, a chart is made of the pattern which is to be used in the border. Figure 127. Secondly, the area which is not required for the edging is coloured.

The third step is to make a new chart of the border by placing only the 'yarn overs' on the graph. Figure 128.

The fourth step is to add the decreases in the right direction to make the chain effect in the border where they outline the holes. Figure 129.

A study of the graph at this stage shows the decreases in some instances to be on the wrong side of the 'yarn overs' to make the execution of the pattern possible. To change them to the other side of the holes would change a major feature of the design.

A solution would be the following: change the decreases to the side where they allow the pattern to work, but reverse the

Figure 128. Versailles border with no decreases.

Figure 129. Redesigned Versailles border with decreases added.

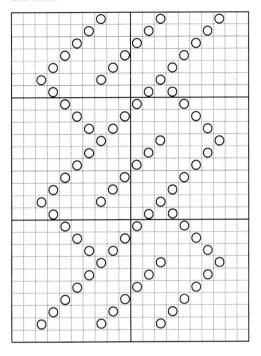

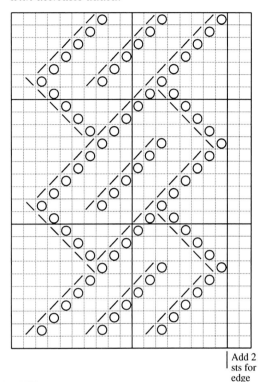

Add 2
sts for
edge

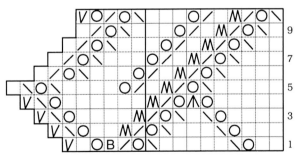

Figure 130. Solution for Versailles border edging.

direction to make them unobtrusive. Then, make a 'mock decrease' on the side of the holes to keep the integrity of the design by introducing a 'make one', or increase into the back of the stitch, next to the 'mock decrease'. Figure 130. This is the technique which can also solve the problem encountered in the exercise, earlier in this Chapter, where a diamond was to be knitted which was to be outlined by the chain effect of the decreases. This is a particularly useful device which gives great facility in reorganising patterns whether traditional, or when designing new ones.

The other solution, which can be learned from the exercises using the diamond shapes at the beginning of this Chapter, is how increases as well as decreases, whether invisible or as a feature of the total pattern, can be used in other parts of the pattern to provide the facility to use features which would otherwise make the design impossible to work.

There will always be limitations on the extent to which actual patterns can be redesigned and still have the appearance intended, simply because of the structure of knitted fabric. For example, faggotting cannot be successfully reproduced in the opposite direction as shown in Figure 131. This is part of the challenge offered to the designer—to work out ways to achieve the wanted results using other alternatives and always to explore new possibilities as one's knowledge increases.

It is important to keep practising these skills. Even when knitting a pattern for which one has no desire at the time to change, be aware of its possibilities. Practise making charts of patterns. It is much easier to work from a chart for a complicated pattern, than to carry around several pages of written instructions.

Use colour pencils to make following a pattern easier. A pattern which is to be repeated many times is much easier to work from if, it is not only enlarged, but also has the alternate row a different colour. This is particularly useful if the alternate row changes from being a pattern row to a plain row, or if it is a

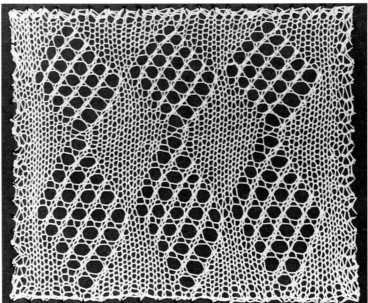

Figure 131. Faggotting and eyelets comparison.

Edward Field

pattern for knitted lace.

From these exercises it should now be possible for the reader to decide on the size and shape of the project of their choice and convert this to a chart 'picture' of the finished piece. Most of the charts have been made showing multiple repeats and also every row in order to make the preceding exercises easier. It is common practice to record only the pattern row of lace knitting, and to show only one full repeat. A solid line indicates any extra stitches required at the beginning and end of the row.

By knitting a series of tension squares, a decision can be made on which yarn, needles and selection of patterns, are going to suit the project.

It should now be possible to make any required adaptations to the selected patterns to conform with the intentions of the designer.

As well as positioning patterns on the chart and deciding the direction for the various pieces to be knitted, all shaping can be plotted and recorded. In other words—a completely unique piece of knitting and the attainment of further skills to ensure success on the next step of the journey!

7. The Big Challenge

ই

Translating sketches into stitches

With the exception of the 'original' patterns I accidentally designed, first as a child misreading patterns and later by once again misunderstanding instructions, as well as by inattention, my early designs were usually minor adjustments to traditional patterns. I had learned from these errors how stitches worked in relation to each other and would often make changes of emphasis in a pattern if I thought it was an improvement. For example, changing the direction in which a decrease was made or making knitted lace instead of lace knitting.

I also had favourite patterns and using basic patterns for garments which I had successfully knitted in the past, I would introduce these patterns to change the appearance of the garment to suit my requirements. A new lesson was learned here when I became aware that a pattern for a stocking-stitch garment tended to be larger when knitted in an all-over lace pattern. However, it was a while before I learned to chart my own adjustments. Instead I tended to knit one of the smaller sizes from the range offered.

Eventually, I became dissatisfied with being limited to only traditional patterns to draw on for providing for a total concept. For example, if I found an all-over pattern I wished to use there never seemed to be a matching edging or vice versa. This led, as described in the previous chapter, to my experimentation with isolating parts of patterns to reorganise them in the form I desired.

At about this time I had reached my goal of spinning and knitting a shawl which I could pull through a wedding ring. It was the response of my husband's family to this shawl, as being 'a most appropriate achievement as the family had originally come from the Shetland Islands', that prompted me to learn more about the knitting of the Shetland Islanders.

The shawl I had knitted, shown in Figure 132, was taken from a booklet of Paton And Baldwin reprints from the United Kingdom, with no alterations to the pattern other than using

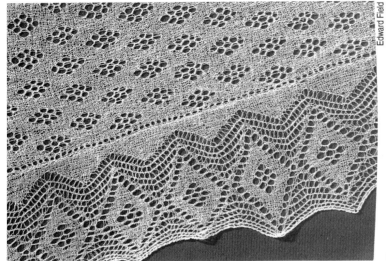

Figure 132. Ring shawl and shawl through a wedding ring.

finer needles. Even changing the needle size from 5.5mm (UK 5, US 9) to 3.25mm (UK 10, US 3) was still not sufficient to make the holes in the centre of the shawl small enough. However, with the help of a fine fabric liner, the shawl has been used successfully without mishap on numerous occasions.

My study of Shetland patterns revealed that they had been adapted and named to reflect the environment where the Shetlanders lived. Even though I was not a Shetland descendant, my children were and so it seemed a good idea to try and find out if there were any family patterns. My enquiries did not bear fruit in this area as it seemed the family had been involved with the fishing industry and there was no record of a lace knitting background. I also discovered that the merino wool I had used to spin my shawl was of quite a different character from the wool used for the Shetland shawls.

I decided instead to bring the tradition full circle and to design a Southern Hemisphere version which reflected the environment in which we lived.

What I really needed now was the motivation to embark on what was a major project, especially as I had a growing family all requiring new knitted garments. A necessity as we lived in such a cold climate!

Two suitable opportunities presented themselves when I received commissions to spin and knit presentation shawls, one for the then Governor General of New Zealand and his wife to celebrate the birth of a grandchild, and the other a vice-regal commission for a cousin of Queen Elizabeth II.

Figure 133. Rata blossom.

Unfortunately, in both instances the time frame allowed for the commissions to be completed, six weeks on both occasions, did not allow the time necessary to invent a new pattern as well.

To prepare myself for any further situations of this nature, and to satisfy my own curiosity as to whether or not I was capable of producing a totally original design, I began experimenting with what was to develop into my Rata pattern.

The Rata blossom, as shown in Figure 133, is a distinctive flower which colours with scarlet the mountain sides of the Otira Gorge side of Arthur's Pass National Park where we were living at the time, and is a native plant of New Zealand. The flower is a cluster of stamens and the leaves are small and slightly curved.

I searched through my various collections of patterns to find shapes similar to those I needed to depict this flower and its leaves. I had never used charts for lace at this stage, even though I used them for Fair Isle knitting. I was also not brave enough to launch out without a 'security blanket'. The patterns I chose on which to base my new design were the 'English Rose Leaf' as in Figure 134 and the 'Cockle Shell', as in Figure 135. I was already very familiar with both of these patterns having knitted them on many occasions.

After numerous samples and much note taking (how much easier a chart would have been!) I eventually worked out how to remove every alternate leaf and replace it with a Rata blossom which was fashioned by using a cluster of long stitches similar to the technique used to make the cockle shells.

This was an exciting development for me and I designed and knitted a circular shawl with a deep border of this Rata pattern. To shape the centre, I decided to carry the leaf motif up beside the decreases, however I decided the motif would be too wide for this purpose. This was solved by using one half of

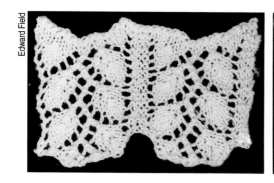

Figure 134. English rose leaf.

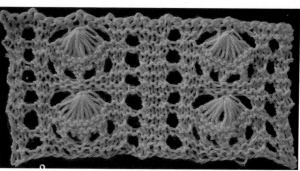

Figure 135. Cockle shell.

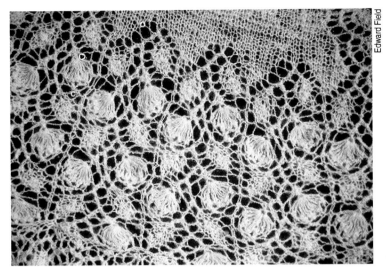

Figure 136. Rata shawl detail.

the full, alternate leaf motif. This led to the idea of finishing the shawl with a border developed from this latter variation. My original intention had been to use the wavy effect created by the design when the shawl was washed and blocked to give an attractive edging, but I felt that the leaf edging was an improvement on this. Figure 136.

Very soon after this, the couple living at a neighbouring high-country sheep station asked me to use their merino fleece to spin and knit a shawl with a New Zealand design. Just what I needed, a strong motivation for surmounting the final hurdle and designing a Rata blossom with Rata leaves, and not borrowed English Rose leaves.

Apart from making drawings, which I then simplified as much as possible to get the shape in my mind, the pattern designing itself was done entirely with needles and yarn. Fortunately, I did not throw away all of these experimentations and Figure 137 gives some idea of the sequence followed in the development of this design.

Even now that I make far more use of graph paper, I still find that, for exploring totally new ideas, I prefer to work with my yarn and needles than with a chart, although I use the latter to record facts as I progress and also I make written instructions hopefully, to cover all contingencies. This is most important when there are constant interruptions.

In my view a shawl should be reversible, which is the reason why I have chosen a garter stitch background. The leaves of the Rata are also designed to look the same from either side.

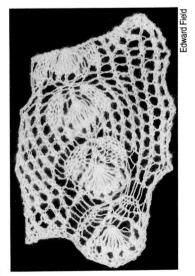

Figure 137. Rata sampler.

105

Figure 138. Rata blossom and shawl designed with Rata blossom pattern.

Stan Jelley

The completed shawl is shown in Figure 138. Once again, I was plagued with problems of keeping control of the size of the open areas, as well as with the distortions which can occur with mesh areas when the effects caused by the decreases in the structure of the lace are not fully appreciated.

Although the result was a step further along the way, it was also a project where I learned a great deal.

I now began to experiment with other flowers and worked on another favourite, the Kowhai blossom, also a native of New Zealand, and one which had special associations for me as, with the exception of Arthur's Pass, it had grown in every place in which I had lived in New Zealand. I think one of my happiest moments was the time when, only a few weeks after arriving in Southland in the beginning of spring when snow was still on the ground, I looked out one morning to see a small Kowhai bush bursting into showers of golden blossom. This was after several years in the far north where Kowhai grew in profusion and we did not even experience a frost! Figure 139.

Figure 140 shows the development of the Kowhai from a basic shape through to the leaves also being included in the design, on this occasion to make the flower reversible, double stocking stitch has been used on a garter-stitch base.

At the top of this photograph is the development of the last of this particular series of flowers which is the Houhere or

Figure 139. Kowhai flowers.

Mountain Ribbonwood. Figure 141. This was one of my most

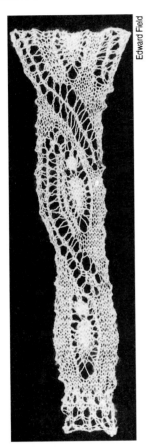

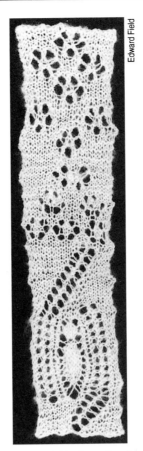

Figure 140. Kowhai sampler.

Figure 141. Completed Kowhai and leaves with Ribbonwood flower sampler at top.

challenging tasks, as this flower has five petals (Figure 141a) and as any knitter knows to make a symmetrical shape of this nature with an uneven number is no easy matter, even if the final result looks quite unspectacular.

Having followed my progress to the point where I was gaining sufficient confidence to use the resources at my disposal to express my own ideas in knitting, let us consider what can be learned from the above projects to assist the reader to achieve similar results.

You have probably already recognised many of the already discussed principles which were used to design these patterns and it now remains to apply them to new shapes and to identify further techniques as they are needed.

As a first exercise to get started make several simple line drawings which may either be representational or quite abstract.

Figure 141a. Ribbonwood flower.

107

Look at your latest doodle and choose a very simple shape from it.

Another really useful hint to get you started is to draw the outline of an object as you look at it, but without looking at the surface on which you are drawing. Pretend your pencil is actually touching the object and that you are tracing around it. This is the technique used by Kimon Nicolaides in his publication *The Natural way to Draw* and is also described in *Drawing from the Right Side of the Brain* by Betty Edwards.

Take the two that you like the best and simplify them as much as possible, accentuating one or two expressive lines. Transfer these lines on to a piece of graph paper, positioning the lines so that they resemble, as closely as possible, your original drawing. Make a border to contain the shape of your design. An example is shown in Figure 142.

Note the angles made by any lines and decide how often the decreases will need to occur to achieve these angles (refer to Chapter 4, Figure 60, page 48). Place the decreases where you think they should go. Now decide where the 'yarn overs' will go to balance these decreases and knit the sample at this stage. Wash and block it and evaluate it, making notes as to how you would like it to be improved.

Your evaluation could include observations and questions similar to the following: perhaps some of the decreases did not need to be close to the 'yarn overs'? Maybe you needed more decrease 'chains' to achieve the angle you wanted? Did you

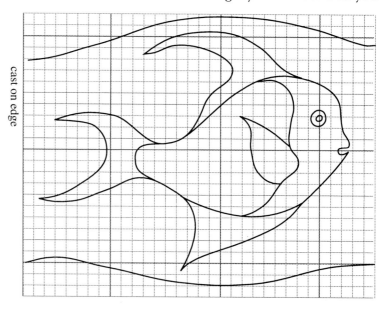

Figure 142. Line drawing.

remember that you could use an invisible increase to allow for this?

Record any possible improvements on another chart and try these out.

Go back to your original drawings—or make fresh ones if desired—and develop three main shapes. Using black, white and grey, colour these shapes. Make a chart with the area you have coloured black as stocking stitch, the white area as an open lace pattern and the grey area as a lace pattern less open than the previous one.

Experiment with different ways of defining each area and record any relevant discoveries. For example, note where a chosen pattern allowed for a necessary decrease, or where the natural bias of a pattern contributed to a design, or perhaps had the opposite effect which needed to be corrected. Any adjustments you make as you knit the samples should be recorded on the relevant chart in a different colour. Resist the temptation to make too many changes at once.

Wash and block the finished samples and evaluate the results. Figure 143.

Figures 144 and 145 show lace interpretations of Argyle and cube patterns. As well as the openwork providing one of the values, there has been an effective use of texture in the use of moss stitch, which contrasts with the smooth stocking-stitch fabric. The decreases have been used to make the linear definition of the argyle diamonds and to outline the cubes.

Figure 143. Three values.

Figure 144. *Lace interpretation of Argyle design.*

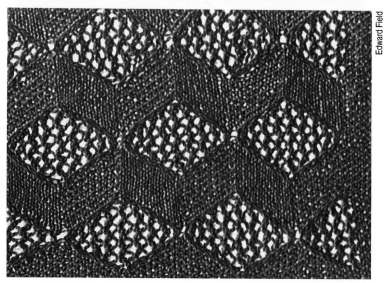

Figure 145. *Lace version of tumbling blocks.*

These two patterns have been devised by Janet Russell of Chicago who has also compiled an index of lace patterns which she updates as new patterns come to her attention.

Make a drawing and then a chart using geometrical shapes similar to those in Figures 144 and 145, and use at least two different openwork patterns of different values in conjunction with solid knitted areas. Use the decreases to 'sharpen' your design.

Figure 146. Moving shapes.

The shapes in many patterns are often helped by the position of the increases and decreases. The shape knitted by itself could be vertical but, by adding stitches to one side of the surrounding fabric and taking them away from the other side, the shape can be moved to give the appearance of a gentle slope on the one hand to an extreme curve on the other as shown in Figure 146.

This technique also produces pointed, scalloped and other shapes to a cast-on and cast-off edge which can be further accentuated in the blocking process. Pinning out these features under tension can give very pleasing effects. The designer must also be aware of this phenomenon when following one of these pattern areas with a plain or balanced fabric and should allow space for this movement to be absorbed, otherwise subsequent shaping may be detrimentally affected.

There are occasions when an idea takes shape which needs to be expressed in a far more complex fashion and for which the techniques covered in the preceding exercises prove to be inadequate. Although the progression is still the same as that which has been already described, the period of experimentation will often take a considerable time and much more ingenuity may be required before the designer arrives at a solution which satisfies.

The most straightforward way to embark on such a challenge is to begin with many drawings of the subject. I generally make the first of these as detailed as possible. Then work on these drawings, simplifying them in different ways, at the same time searching for the best use of line and mass to express the essence of the idea. Figure 147.

Figure 147. Drawings of Rata and Kowhai.

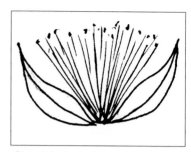

Simplified version.

Rata flower.

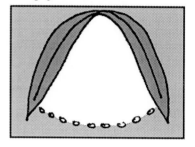

In direction of knitting.

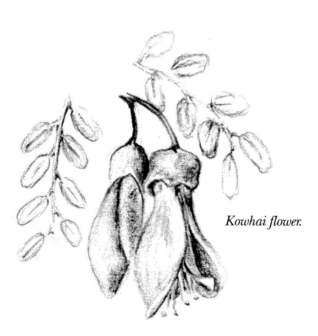

Kowhai flower.

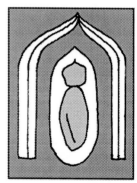

Simplified version.

In direction of knitting.

Sometimes it helps, after a rest period, to draw the design from memory. This is a valuable exercise to assist in discarding what is unnecessary, as the memory forgets distracting details and tends to retain the elements of the design which attracted you to it in the first place.

Finally make a drawing with as few values as possible and isolate one element and devise a way of describing it in knitting. It is wise to choose the one you feel you can resolve easily, so that you have something to build on. You may wish to make a chart immediately, or you may prefer to work with a combination of knitting, written notes and a chart.

Once you are pleased with a result then record this and start on another aspect of the design, first of all on its own and then, when you think it is ready, begin plotting out how the two parts of the design can interrelate with one another. Work through the rest of the design in the same way.

At this stage there should not be any importance attached to consistency in the number of stitches in each row, as it is more important to ensure the visual effects are correct. Once this is achieved, then the whole piece can be translated to a chart and a study made of the places where stitches may be reorganized to reconcile the row by row stitch numbers and to fine tune the overall design.

Reference to Figures 137 and 140 will show the progression which took place for my New Zealand, native flower series. It should be noted that each one starts with a very simple shape and changes are introduced one at a time. The other important feature to note with these samplers is that the progression is maintained and not unravelled as an improved solution is tried.

During the workshops I have taught on this subject I have noticed that, with few exceptions, it is an almost automatic response, when working towards a solution, to unravel each attempt before starting the next one. I regard my samplers much as a sketch pad. There will be successful as well as unsatisfactory results. However, each attempt will be adding new understanding and it is desirable to be able to look back and constantly evaluate progress by comparing the current version with what has gone before.

The sampler also preserves results which, with further development in a different direction, can become useful components for future designs. An example of this is the last of the experiments for the Kowhai blossom in Figure 140. This version was too pointed to be used as a Kowhai in my opinion

*Figure 148. Kakabeak flower
from drawing to initial pattern.*

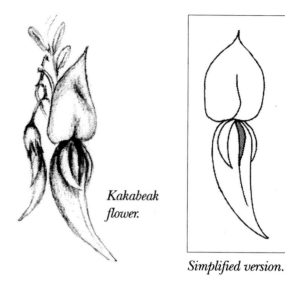

*Kakabeak
flower.*

Simplified version.

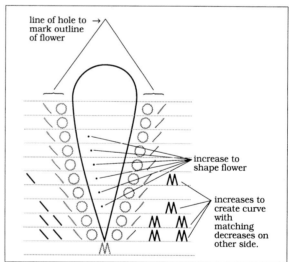

and I chose the one below it. However, it lends itself to be developed into a Kakabeak flower as shown in Figure 148.

To do this, the techniques I would employ would be to introduce extra stitches on one side and decrease a corresponding number on the other, to curve the point of the flower to one side and then work out a petal to complete the fully open flower.

The following is a description of the development of the rosebud design which is used in the pattern for the curtain in Appendix E.

Several years ago a special friend had asked me to devise a pattern of a rose for a baby bonnet. I had never managed to produce one with which I was satisfied. This was probably because I had always tried to use a full blown rose as my subject. The results had always looked too clumsy for a baby, so eventually I decided a bud would be more appropriate. As well as making several drawings of a rosebud from my garden I also photographed it. I then simplified the drawing until I felt I had the shapes which, in my view, best portrayed the representation of the rosebud.

The next decision was to identify any parts of the design which I felt I could immediately express in knitting. This was the stem, as I had been recently knitting a pattern which used the technique of slipping two stitches, one at a time, then knitting the next stitch on the left-hand needle and then passing the two slipped stitches over that stitch. This resulted in holding the central stitch in position and creating a vertical chain effect. The abbreviation for this technique is 'sl 2 k1 p2sso' and the chart symbol /I\.

The next part was to make the ovule, the rounded shape below the sepals. This indicated an increase in the number of stitches, but keeping the line of the stem intact and also keeping the two continuously linked. Usual methods of knitting several stitches into one stitch result in a hole being formed, because the stitch is stretched to accommodate the extra stitches. For this reason I decided to reinforce the area where the extra stitches were to be made and based the increase technique on that used for making the stem. Instead of knitting once into the stitch on the left-hand needle before passing the two slipped stitches over, I knitted three times into that stitch and then passed the two slipped stitches over all three new stitches. The 'yarn overs' on either side were balanced by decreases on each side from the background area.

The above was the final solution, however I tried several other ways of creating the required effect before discovering this one. The first was to make a stocking-stitch 'bobble' which was unsuitable as it appeared separate from the stem. The second was to knit three together but, before removing the three stitches from the left-hand needle, I purled and then knitted into the three stitches again to make three stitches. I used this as an interim solution as shown in the bottom example on the sampler in Figure 149.

By now, I was beginning to rough out a possible chart and,

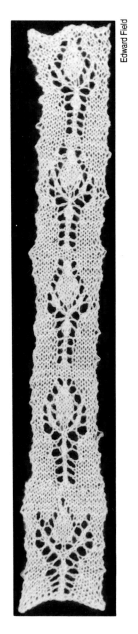

Figure 149. Rosebud sampler.

Edward Field

115

as I was thinking of possible solutions to the sepals and bud, I continued knitting a temporary shape, doing this ensured that I did not forget these ideas before I reached the stage when I was going to need them. It also helped me to keep the proportions of the subject correct.

Although the rosebud shape is probably recognisable in this first attempt, it did not match up to my expectations and, going back to my drawings, I reviewed the lines and shapes which I felt needed to be fine tuned in the knitted version.

I decided to concentrate on improving the sepals and the unfolding effect of the petals. This led to the decrease / increase technique used to shape the sepals and to slipping a stitch over several for the top of the bud. It was working on these two methods which finally led me to the solution I used for the ovule.

Whilst I was working on the sampler, I was also writing notes and remaking the chart and, when I was satisfied with the rosebud, I then turned my attention to the background. As I had chosen a diamond shape for the frame, I positioned this on the chart and made the necessary adjustments for balancing out stitch numbers. Figure 150.

To use this motif as an all-over pattern presented a problem in that the half pattern, which a diamond grid would create, was going to be most unattractive. I also felt that a rosebud in every grid could be too busy and that a pattern for leaf shapes in alternate diamonds would be far more attractive.

With Herbert Neibling as my rôle model, I decided to make up a chart for leaves, since I had all the specifications I should have needed. I counted off the squares and superimposed a drawing of the leaves I had visualised. What I thought would be a simple exercise proved to be a disaster, as can be seen in Figures 151 and 152!

Finally it was back to my old method of using yarn, needles, written notes and chart and I have discovered, while teaching my workshops, that those who can work exclusively with charts are few and far between. It is far more common for people to need to use the practical knitting processes to get the results they want. No doubt the more practice one has the more one's expertise in this area will improve but, for myself, I still have a long way to go before I can be confident in working exclusively with a chart and its symbols.

Whilst putting the two charts together and knitting the complete pattern, it occurred to me that, with such deep

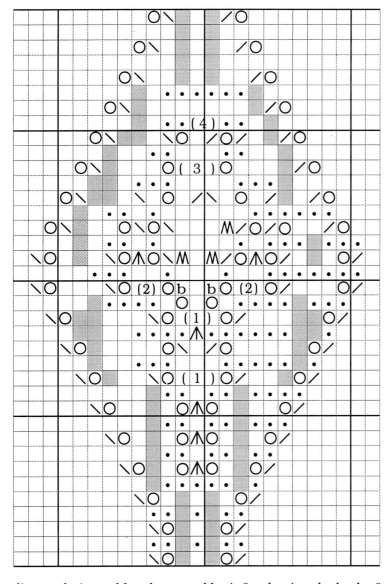

Figure 150. Rosebud in diamond.

diamonds, it would make a good basis for shaping the back of the bonnet and so my first project using this design can be seen in Figure 153.

I have used this design for the curtain in my kitchen and the pattern is that given in Appendix E.

As with painting a picture, a teacher cannot give a formula for success, only share knowledge—acquired and added to over the years—of using materials and techniques and then, by employing this accumulated experience, to equip students to not only recognise and make use of their own and other

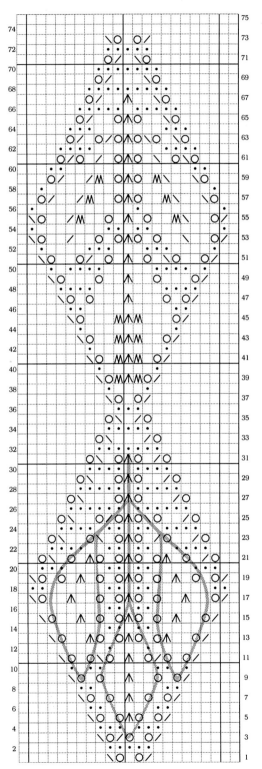

Figure 152. Development of leaf shapes.

Figure 151. Leaf sampler.

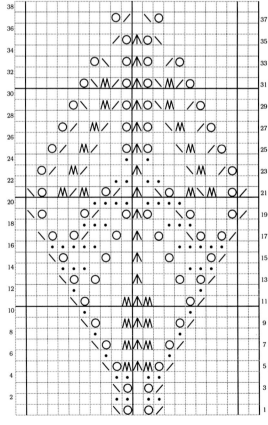

Edward Field

Figure 152a. Solution A.

Figure 153. Rosebud bonnet.

resources, but also to motivate them to express their own creative ideas.

It is my personal belief that 'craft' becomes a truly individual expression when the artist can leave reliance on patterns and formulae behind, and can confidently draw on the wealth of experience gained through practical experimentation, constant self-evaluation and participation in the activities and developments of the wider craft community.

Bearing this in mind, the examples used in this book, where artwork has been translated into lace and the steps through which this transition took place, are included to illustrate one person's solution to a creative challenge. A good example of what I wish to express is the one I use in my workshops.

If each student were to write a letter 'A' on the blackboard, there would be no two 'A's which would be completely identical. Yet we would all recognise the letter and it would have some meaning beyond mere identification for each person viewing it. In a similar way each student in a class with the same materials, the same instructor and topic, should produce a result which is unique to them for no other reason than that they are themselves unique, and their achievement can only be measured in relation to the place they have reached on their own particular 'journey'.

8. 'Sea Spray and Scallop Shells'

❧

A project from inspiration to accomplishment

This chapter aims to give the reader a step by step example of how understanding the structure of lace that is knitted and being able to make use of yarn grist, needle size and the information provided by samples as discussed in the preceding chapters, can be employed to provide solutions to the problems arising from translating an original design into a finished piece.

The project being described here is a shawl which makes use of as many of the techniques which have been discussed in the previous chapters as possible. I find that a considerable length of time can elapse from the first inspiration to getting a definite shape down on paper. It can often be the already referred to 'doodle' which will be the first stage of the design taking shape, even though I have been thinking about it for some time. On other occasions, the idea is ready to take shape almost immediately and then it is very important, as these are the designs which can often be lost if not recorded immediately, to get it on to paper straight away. Designs which are commissioned are usually in a different category, as there are specifications to work to and it is likely to be a bonus if the requested design links up with an idea currently being explored.

The ideas and designs for this particular shawl evolved over a period of time. It was seeing an attractive swirling pattern, used for the centre of a doily which made me think of sea spray. I used this pattern, substituting garter stitch for the stocking stitch used in the doily, as a model for a shawl intended for a friend and, whilst I was working the design, I was intrigued by other possible variations which could be worked. Some preliminary drawings and seashore visits resulted in a simple drawing which showed exciting possibilities, as shown in Figure 154. Although I continued to think about it, at this stage the drawing was put aside as I pursued other commitments.

It was two years later that I looked at the drawing again as a

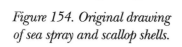

Figure 154. Original drawing of sea spray and scallop shells.

design to knit for an exhibition and I actually started knitting the centre from superfine, handspun yarn. However, as I had not been able to decide how to create the area between the centre and the scallop shell border, other than that I wanted to use seaweed which included 'Neptune's Necklace', it was put aside and later the yarn used for another project.

In the meantime, I was able to avail myself of opportunities to explore different fibres and dye methods which had the effect of broadening the scope of what I could incorporate in my designs. The traditional interpretation of the type of work I had been doing required white or natural yarn, for example the colour of the fibre as it grows on the animal, or plant, without added dye or bleaching.

Most commissions still tend to be conservative in this respect, which means any major experimentation with colour is mainly restricted to work for the family and exhibitions. Consequently, the final interpretations for the shawl, as a gift for my daughter, allowed me to break with tradition and experiment with the new resources at my disposal.

My final reservations relating to the use of colour were finally dispelled when our local guild organised a 'Theory of Colour' workshop, tutored by Michael Reid at the Christchurch Polytechnic, a course designed especially for craftspeople working with fibre. This was just the extra motivation I needed to get a final design together and to test out my ideas. The artwork which resulted from the course is shown in Figure 155.

Figure 155. Coloured version.

Figure 156. Dyed roving.

Although I was still not completely satisfied with the shapes and colours for the seaweed section, a start had been made and I began collecting seaweed and making observational drawings which, eventually, gave me the shapes I wanted. Figure 156.

The next stage was to take each section and find a solution for translating that part into yarn and lace which would best express the intended idea and which would, at the same time keep in mind the harmony of the total statement.

The centre of the shawl which was the sea with sunlight sparkling on it, was the first task that I set myself. For this I used my English-style wool combs to comb several merino wool rovings which I dyed, starting with a very pale blue for the centre and gradually deepening the colour and introducing enough yellow to give a strong sea-green for the last part. To judge how much to dye of each colour I made a 'guesstimate' using Elizabeth Zimmerman's pi-shawl theory where the number of stitches are doubled on the round on which the increases are made and the number of rounds without increasing are doubled between each of the increase rounds.

I reached a more accurate estimate of the amount of yarn required by measuring off a 30 centimetre piece of the roving (one foot) and spinning a length of yarn from it which was measured and then knitted, starting at the centre of the shawl. I was able to work out the yardage required for the centre section (by calculating how many stitches could be knitted from that length) and what lengths of the combed roving needed to be dyed in the different shades of blue and blue/green. This

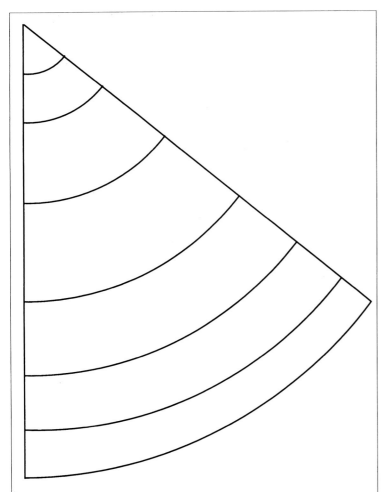

Notes for Figure 157.

Calculations for shading the colours in the shawl centre.

Radius 5cm (2ins) = 20 rounds, 12.8 metres (14yds).
For centre - 7cm = 25m required of palest blue.
For first band - 10cm = 123m required of pale blue.
For second band - 12cm = 283m required of blue.
For third band - 9cm = 308m required of blue/blue/green.
For fourth band - 7cm = 300m required of blue/green/green.
For fifth band - 5cm = 241m required of green.

Figure 157. Calculations, drawing and yarn.

washed and blocked sample also provided me with confirmation of how many rows depth of knitting I needed for each area of colour. It can be very useful if you can enlist family members who have good mathematical skills, even if it is only to confirm the results which have been calculated. Figure 157.

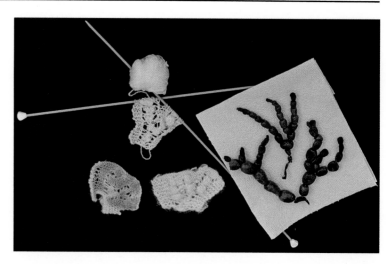

*Figure 158. Neptune's necklace
and sea spray.*

To achieve the 'sparkle' of the sun on the water, I spun a single of silk with a slight irregularity which was then plyed with a single spun from the dyed merino. This was then knitted in the spiral pattern. Garter stitch was used to give the texture of waves.

The easy part was now over! Next was solving the problem of the seaweed, 'Neptune's Necklace'.

'Neptune's Necklace' seemed a most appropriate transition from ocean to shoreline, as it formed the opposite image from that which the arrangement of holes expressing the sea spray created. Where there had been holes in the earlier design there were now 'bobble' shapes 'floating on the foam' which continued the circular movement. Figure 158.

To give the effect of wet seaweed I decided to continue to use silk combined with the merino wool. However, now I had the problem of having alternating areas of sea and seaweed which were different colours and I did not wish to use an intarsia method. I also wanted to be economical with time. I decided to spin the yarn for this part of the shawl undyed as a two-fold yarn of one single of silk and one of merino wool and complete the knitting of the seaweed section. The plan being that, when the knitting of the whole shawl was completed, a cold-batch-dye method would be used to apply appropriate colour to the various elements in this part of the design.

This scheme had an added advantage in that it allowed the total shawl to be made in yarn of uniform construction, thus eliminating any problems which may have arisen from areas being knitted from yarns with different properties, for example, elasticity. I was also going to achieve the effect of 'wetness' from the sheen provided by the silk being coloured in conjunction with the wool.

After working on many possible solutions for the 'beads' of the 'Neptune's Necklace', I eventually decided on a double-stocking-stitch version to continue the reversible fabric of the shawl and turned the design up the opposite way from that which had featured in my original concept. The sections of the pattern were divided off, as shown in Figure 159.

The stages of creating this design began with making samplers first of 'bobble' patterns, as given in knitting books. The needle size and grist of the yarn resulted in 'beads' which lacked substance in relation to the background fabric. This led to the double-stocking-stitch version and an appropriate number of stitches decided on to give suitable dimensions in accordance with the size required for the various sections. The branching of the lines of 'beads' was the part of the design to be solved, together with the size of the surrounding holes.

Paying close attention to the detail of the tiny segments—and thinking of them as stitches—actually gave me helpful clues when it came to 'fine tuning' the placement of increases and decreases to create the form of the seaweed, especially where the branching occurred.

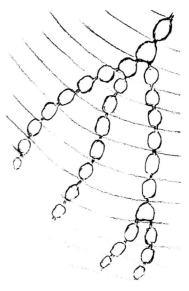

Figure 159. Neptune's necklace divisions.

To knit the insertion featuring the bladder kelp (*Macrocystis pyrifera*), I decided to change the direction of the knitting. This allowed the shape of the seaweed to be outlined with a chain stitch and also accentuated the trailing effect. The stitches for the insertion were cast on, using crochet cotton which was later unravelled after sliding a finer needle through the stitches of the first pattern row. These stitches could then be grafted to the last row of the insertion.

The bladder kelp was probably the easiest of the motifs to express. After making drawings from collected samples and composing the position of the kelp in the border as shown in Figure 160, the sample knitting began. The bladder was worked in double-stocking-stitch which provided a repetition of the technique used in the 'Neptune's Necklace' ensuring the total design was in harmony, and a chain of decreases adjacent to a 'yarn over' was used to connect each section to the main branch, the latter also being made in this manner. The ribbon-like section trailing from the bladder was outlined in chain stitch and holes and the 'ribbons' of the seaweed, which are translucent and have a rippled effect brought about by varying thicknesses, was expressed by using an elongated broken rib.

125

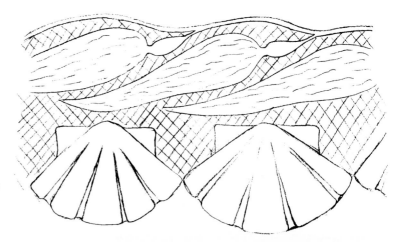

Figure 160. Kelp drawings and arrangements.

Figure 161. Samplers with kelp arrangements.

This also continued the reversible nature of the fabric. Figure 161 shows samples knitted to construct the final pattern for this section.

Using the white merino and silk yarn, the insertion was knitted on to the stitches of the centre of the shawl. I allowed one stitch to be worked off for each two rows of the insertion. However, in retrospect I have decided that this was too great an increase to allow for the seaweed pattern to be blocked to the best advantage and it would have improved the flow of the design had the stitches at the circumference of the 'Neptune's Necklace' section of the shawl been decreased by about one sixth.

To complete the shawl, a border of scallop shells surrounded and edged by sea foam, was knitted on to stitches picked up along the edge of the border. The wool for this part of the shawl was dyed as a random pink and mauve with some white wool and spun as a variegated yarn from the staple. It was then plyed with undyed silk.

The pattern for the scallop shells was not as straightforward as my imagination had suggested. This was partly due to the softness and draping quality of the yarn I had chosen. The use of double-stocking-stitch proved to be unsuitable in my opinion as it was too thick for the effect I wanted and looked clumsy. As a result I settled for a solution which also resulted in expressing the two sides of the shell with quite realistic accuracy.

By using stocking stitch for the upper side of the shell and defining the vertical furrows by using a purl stitch, I was also able to achieve the effect, as it appears in nature, of the underside of the shell. Altogether a most satisfactory result. However, it was considerable trial and error which eventually led to the almost invisible increase in the width of the fan shape of the shell and, by using the 'short rows' technique, the scallop shape was formed. Figure 162.

My only real regret about the shell pattern for this project was the fact that the yarn did not have, as I had originally intended, sufficient bulk to hold the rounded shape of the shell. Another project and another challenge!

Figure 163 shows a section of the completed shawl after being washed and blocked and before the dye was introduced to the seaweed border, and Figure 164 shows the application of the

Figure 162. Samplers of scallop shell development.

127

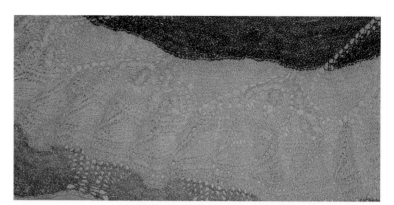

Figure 163. Undyed section of border.

Figure 164. Dyeing process.

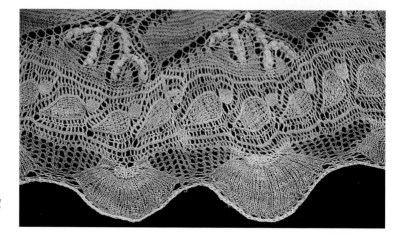

Figure 165. Detail of dyed border.

dye. This was applied while the shawl was blocked under tension and the colours and technique were tried out on samples first, but in every other way the dyeing was carried out in much the same way as a water-colour painting. This process has endless possibilities and local suppliers of craft dyes will undoubtedly be able to assist the reader in finding a suitable product for this type of exercise. Figure 165.

For a project of this nature, spinners have the advantage of being able to design and produce the exact yarn that they require, however if the non-spinner does not have a friend accomplished in these skills, there are still many different ways in which original yarns can be obtained by dyeing and mixing two or more different yarns, fibres, fabrics and other materials. It is not always necessary to twist them together before knitting.

Although I had made the decision, at the time of the Theory of Colour Workshop, to make this shawl for my younger daughter and also to describe the process of its construction as a chapter for this book, another motivating force presented itself with my daughter's announcement that she was expecting her first baby. I am sure that this also had a final influence on how the pattern was composed and, as an example of how many factors can contribute to a project, I include here the dedication which accompanied the shawl which became a gift for my granddaughter, Michaela.

A Shawl for Michaela
'Sea Spray and Scallop Shells'

'The idea for this shawl goes back many years to when we lived at Arthur's Pass and our annual excursion to the sea—usually Totaranui in Abel Tasman National Park—was an experience in sharp contrast to the rigours of our alpine climate. The sun sparkling on the water, 'popping' seaweed and collecting scallops for tea were enjoyed by our whole family.

'Your mother, Kristine (named after her great great grandmother, a spinner and knitter who came to New Zealand from Aarhus in Denmark as an eighteen year old), was born in Hokianga and has returned to Northland several times, both on holiday and later with your father, to work. Their full-time employment in the ski industry over the last few years has meant they still value time spent in a seaside environment when the opportunity arises.

'Your father, Chance Sullivan, belongs to the Ngati

Tuwharetoa tribe of Taupo and your ancestors arrived in the Te Arawa canoe which landed at Makatu. Your great-grandmother, Selina Sullivan, lives at Te Awanga, in Hawkes Bay, a small seaside settlement, and this is where your father spent much of his childhood.

'The fibres which I have spun for your shawl are superfine merino wool, which has been grown in the New Zealand high country, and silk from Japan. Your father has worked two Northern Hemisphere winters in Japan and during his last trip was joined by your mother who returned to New Zealand two months before your birth so that you could be born in Aotearoa (New Zealand).

'The spiral of the sea spray is based on a very early design used in circular knitting. It was necessary to work out the approximate yardage of each shade of the blues, through turquoise into green, which was achieved by working samples and enlisting your grandfather's mathematical expertise. The wool was dyed in the fleece and blended on English-style wool combs to give a true worsted preparation. The wool and silk were spun as individual singles and then plied together so that the silk would give the impression of the sun sparkling on the water.

'The border of scallop shells was clear in my mind, right from the beginning, however it took some time for the turbulence at the water's edge to clear sufficiently for the 'Neptune's Necklace' to appear and it was a walk along Sumner beach with your cousin Nathaniel which led to the discovery of the *Macrocystis* (bladder kelp) for the border.

'As I wanted to create the effect of shiny, wet seaweed, I knitted the seaweed areas in merino plyed with silk which had not been dyed and later painted this area with cold batch dyes. The shells were knitted from yarn where the wool had been dyed pink in a range of intensities and then spun from prepared staples which were plyed with silk. White was once again used for a border of foam.

'Each of the pattern units were developed separately. The 'Neptune's Necklace' was based on a bobble stitch, but used double-knit fabric. Double knit was also used for the 'bubble' of *Macrocystis*, with the ribbon-like part expressed in a broken rib to simulate the ripple effect; this also kept it reversible and translucent.

'The shells have ribs which look very like those that occur naturally. In fact, when there was difficulty working out stitch numbers and placement of stitches, studying the solutions reached by nature invariably led to the answer'. Figure 166.

Edward Field

Figure 166. Finished shawl.

The purpose of this book has been to provide the knitter with a wide range of options as the result of an increased understanding of the structure of hand-knitted fabric: an understanding which is reinforced by a series of graded exercises and challenges to take the reader to a stage where a positive approach can be taken to creating original designs. For practical reasons, this has been based on experimentation and the extention of a basic range of knitting techniques used and understood by the majority of knitters.

However, the intention of this book is also to encourage knitters to continue experimentation and to pursue further research into the methods and solutions achieved by others. By demonstrating how I have used a variety of sources to form the basis of my experimentation, in conjunction with new ideas which have evolved as the need for a particular solution became apparent, I hope that, the reader seeking inspiration, will also be encouraged to make similar use of the wealth of already published material.

Although the reader may be satisfied at this stage with the range of skills already achieved, there are many variations on even the way stitches are formed and, at some time, this information may be very useful. The bibliography provided in Appendix B should be a good start for those who are ready to extend their knowledge.

As just a small example, take the 'yarn over' technique which has been used in this book, one which creates a loop that follows the direction of the stitches both preceding and following it. This ensures that the following row has a loop which presents the right side of the loop on the side of the needle facing the knitter, and the left side of the loop on the far side, or behind the needle in relation to the knitter. This can be very simply changed to produce the reverse effect, as shown in the following method of producing a stocking-stitch fabric.

Figure 167. Twisted stocking-stitch.

This version of a stocking-stitch fabric which is not comprised of twisted stitches as shown in Figure 167, is made simply by turning all the stitches so that the right side of the stitch is on the far side of the needle. This is achieved by bringing the yarn under instead of over the needle when knitting. Use of this technique immediately leads to the possibilities of providing a 'mirror image' for design elements.

Mary Thomas's Knitting Book and June Hemmons Hiatt's *The Principles of Knitting* provide very clear instructions and illustrations of the various structural changes obtained by needle position and yarn direction.

The more one understands how the structure of knitting works, the easier it is to make adjustments to one's personal knitting techniques, either for speed or comfort, which do not compromise the integrity of the result.

A good project to mark this first milestone of your 'creative knitting' journey—and to introduce you to the wealth of information in your library and perhaps to utilize what is already on your bookshelves—is to make samples of as many different cast-on edgings as you can find. Use different yarns, as in earlier samples described in Chapter 3, and record your comments on their suitability, or otherwise, for various projects.

Also, make a similar series of cast-off edges and evaluate these as well.

With these signposts, it is now up to you to decide on and enjoy the as yet uncharted space between casting on and casting off!

Appendix A

❧

Abbreviations, chart symbols, construction and finishing techniques

Abbreviations and symbols used for the patterns in *Creating Original Hand-knitted Lace.*

k   **knit**

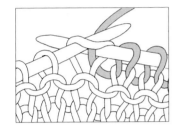

p   **purl**

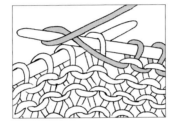

st   **stitch**

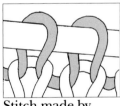

Stitch made by above methods.

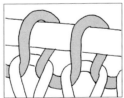

Turned stitch. Yarn wrapped in opposite direction.

tbl   **through back of loop**

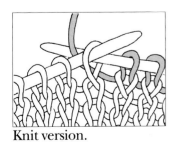

Knit version.

Purl version.

b   **back.**

Optional abbrev. for tbl.

inc   **increase**

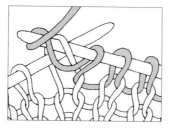

(K1, p1) in 1 stitch.

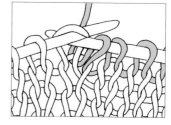

K1, in the row below then knit the stitch on the needle.

incB   **knit into front then back of st.**

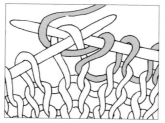

Knit version.

Purl version.

dec   **decrease** Work 2 or more sts together.

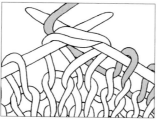

K2 tog.

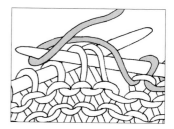

P2 tog.

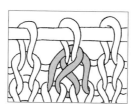

position of stitches when completed.

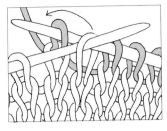

Sl 1, k1, psso.

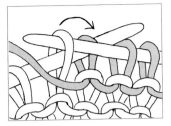

P1 and transfer back to left-hand needle, sl st to left of p1 and psso the p1, transfer to right-hand needle.

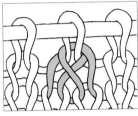

position of stitches when completed.

rep   **repeat**

alt   **alternate**

sl   **slip a st.**   **rsl**   **slip a st to reverse.**

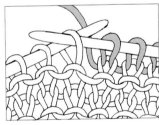

As if to purl.

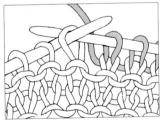

As if to knit (reverses st).

psso   **pass slipped st over.**

sl 2   **slip 2 sts as if to knit together.**

p2sso   **pass 2 slipped sts over.**

tog   **together.**

ssk   slip, slip, knit   **ssp   purl version of ssk**

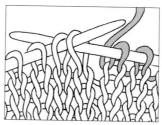 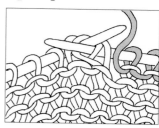

Slip, slip, knit, by slipping 2 sts one at a time from left needle on to right needle then, placing left needle through the slipped sts and knitting them.

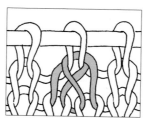

position of stitches when completed.

yo   yarn over

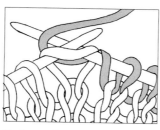 

Knit version.   Purl version.

m1   make 1

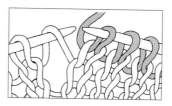 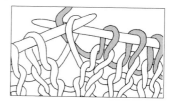

Make one by lifting thread from row below which runs between two stitches and then knitting into back of loop.

m1o   make 1

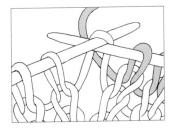

Make one as above, but knit into front of loop.

st st   stocking stitch—1 row knit, 1 row purl.

g st   garter stitch—every row knit.

wyib   with yarn carried behind.

wyif   with yarn carried in front.

dr   drop stitch without knitting it.

hs   horizontal stitch *attributed to the late Trude Guermonprez*

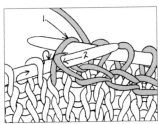

IncB in st which precedes first horizontal stitch to be worked (increased st becomes hs) * rsl first st on left-hand needle, sl hs on to left needle, k1 in far side of rsl, k1 in hs. Rep. from *. To complete k hs and next st tog.

phso   pass horizontal st over.

Chart Symbols.

Worked from right side.	From wrong side.
☐ k1	p1
• p1	k1
b k1 tbl	p1 tbl
↓ k1 in st of row below.	p1 in st of row below.
૪ k1 elongated—by wrapping yarn over needle twice.	p1 elongated—as for k1 elongated.
૪૪ k1 elongated twice—wrap yarn over needle 3 times.	p1 elongated twice—as for k1 elongated twice.
	sl 1 wyib	sl 1 wyif
— sl 1 wyif	sl 1 wyib
▨ no stitch	no stitch
O yo	yo
OO (yo) twice. On next row k1, p1 or incB into double loop.	(yo) twice. As for right side.
M m1	
V inc	inc
B incB	incB
∕ k2 tog	p2 tog
∖ ssk or k2 tog tbl, or sl 1, k1, psso.	ssp or p2 tog tbl or p1, return to left needle, pass st to left over p1 and return to right-hand needle.

⟋.	p2 tog		k2 tog
⟍	p2 tog tbl or ssp		k2 tog tbl or ssk
∧	sl 1, k2 tog, psso for left slant. Ssk, return and pass st to left over ssk for right slant.		p2 tog return new st to left needle, pass st to left over p2 tog for left slant. Sl 1 wyif, p2 tog, psso for right slant.
⋀	k3 tog		p3 tog
⋀	k3 tog tbl or sssk		p3 tog tbl or sssp
⋀	p3 tog		k3 tog
⋀	p3 tog tbl		k3 tog tbl
⋀	sl 2, k1, p2sso		sl 2 tbl, p1, p2sso
⟩	hs		

Where special instructions are required a numeral, for example (1), is included with that chart.

There are other variations for both increasing and decreasing than those given above. The important point to be aware of when deciding which method to use, is to look at the finished position of all the stitches and use the method which enhances the design. The way the result is accomplished does not really matter as long as it is the easiest and quickest and most practical way for the knitter. The above instructions are those most commonly used and provide a good foundation.

When translating written instructions to chart form, begin with a row by row version and then, if necessary, centre the pattern and re-chart. Where repeats occur between asterisks, allow squares for the greatest number of stitches on each side and use 'no stitch' squares where necessary to balance stitch numbers.

When recording a pattern which is to be used by others and where a yarn other than that used for the original may need to be substituted, it is necessary to give a tension measurement in order that the article may be reproduced with the same measurements as the original. As there may be considerable variation over the article, depending on the patterns used in the design, it is customary to give a measurement over stocking stitch as shown in the diagram, using the yarn and needles recommended for the pattern and any special comments noted.

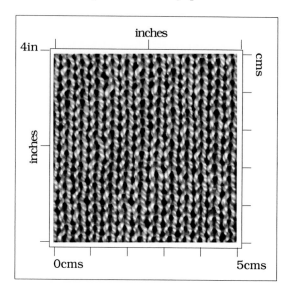

Figure 168. Measuring Tension.

Details on how to gain information and measurements from tension squares are given in Chapter 5. However, to complete tension squares they need to be finished in the same way as the planned project will later be finished. Basically there are two methods. For garments or pieces which have textured areas which are designed to have a degree of elasticity, as in ribbed bands, cables and other forms of surface pattern, the finishing would take the form of easing into shape on a flat surface after washing by using a method suited to the type of yarn used. The amount of tension or stretch would be limited to that which is required to open up the lacy areas.

For very lacy pieces, particularly those where the pattern relies on the contrast between the open areas and solid fabric for the design to work, it will be necessary to pin the edges out under more tension. The amount of tension will once again depend on the yarn used and what is appropriate for the particular design.

As the squares are not likely to be very large, these can be pinned out on a flat padded surface and adjusted until the desired result is achieved.

When the project is eventually completed, initial calculations made for the finished size will enable a pattern to be made as a guide for pinning it out. Ease into shape to begin with and then gradually increase the tension required evenly over the whole piece, rather than completing one section at a time. An example is shown in the accompanying diagram.

Steaming, ironing or pressing if required, will be in accordance with the yarn used and the instructions of the manufacturer of the product.

The amount of yarn required can also be estimated by working a square from a measured length of the yarn. The number of stitches divided by the number of metres (yards) equals the number of stitches per metre (yard). The number

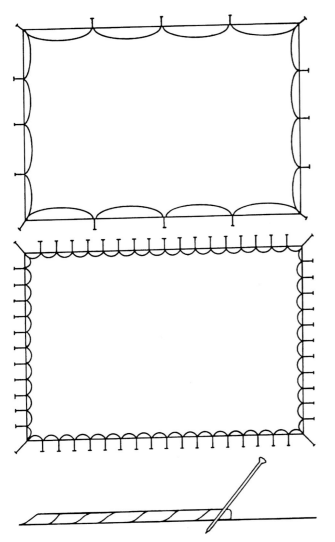

Figure 169. Pinning out edges under tension.

Knitted piece pinned to shape.

Pinning completed with piece stretched to optimum size.

Angle of pin in relation to the fabric.

of stitches per 5cm (2ins) multiplied by the number of rows per 5cm (2ins) equals the number of stitches per square 5cm (2ins). The number of stitches per square 5cm (2ins) divided by the number of stitches per metre (yard) is equal to the number of metres (yards) per square 5cm (2ins). The total number of square 5cm (2ins) in the article being made can be determined by calculation directly from a prepared graph or a scale diagram. Fortunately most yarns today are sold with the length recorded on the label which makes it much easier to purchase the correct amount.

In this next section I have included samples from several charting systems. It is interesting to note how some symbols are common to most of them, or have only minor differences. The more complex the designs, the more sophisticated the symbols become. The symbols used by Herbert Neibling in *Burda* magazine reflect the intricte designs for which he is famous, however these symbols are difficult and laborious to make for the knitter who is charting by hand. Some of the systems work well where the designs are relatively simple, but once more complex variations are required the options become very limited. Others do not have a provision for a patterned purl row.

There can even be differences in the technique referred to in some of the abbreviations which are used and this can be a trap for the unwary. A prime example of this is the abbreviation 'm' for 'make'. In many early pattern books published in England, 'make' is synonymous with 'yarn over', 'wool forward' and 'wool over needle'. This use of 'make' appears in late eighteenth century publications such as *Weldon's Practical Knitter*, published by Weldons Ltd, London and *Needlecraft—Knitted Edgings*, published by the Manchester School of Embroidery. Later, it is used in the *Bestway* pattern books, The Amalgamated Press Ltd, London, the publications of Vyella House, William Hollins and Company Ltd, London, and it is also used in many of the *Australian Home Journal* pattern books and, as late as 1963, this usage appears in the English translation of *Mon Tricot*. A more recent *Mon Tricot* publication uses 'yarn over' instead and does not list 'm' or 'make' at all. It is, therefore, most important to check the abbreviations AND the technique for which it stands in each new publication.

Below I have included some examples from a variety of charting systems to demonstrate the differences which one may encounter when using other versions, and why it is important to be aware of their particular advantages and disadvantages as these need to be evaluated when deciding on your special requirements when you come to choose symbols for recording your own designs.

Abbreviations *	Christine Duchrow•	Marie Niedner••	Burda	Marianne Kinzel	Knitters' Magazine	Susanna Lewis	Neue Mode	Rachel Schnelling	Mary Thomas	Babara G. Walker	Japanese Version
K1	r	■	■	▮	▯	□	•	K	⌴	□	▯
p1	l	⊟	⊟	▬	—	▨	▬	P	■	·	—
K1 tbl	ⱴ	◆	◆	▪			Ø	B	✕	B	Ⴑ
p1 tbl			◇				ⵁ		⊠		
yo	1	O	O	O	O		U	I	●	O	O
sl 1 wyib			▯	✚	V	ⱽ			⌐	▯	V
sl 1 wyif			Ø			ⱴ			⌐	—	ⱴ
inc	rr	V	U		Y		⊔		⊕	V	
K2 tog	g	◣	◣	⟋	⟋	⟋	⟋	T	⋀	⟋	⟋
ssk	a	◣	◣	⟍	⟍	⟍	⟍	D	⋔	⟍	⟍
sl 1 k2 tog psso	3	◭	⌂	⋀	⋏	⋏	⋀	3	⋔	⋀	⋏
sl 2 k1 p2sso			⌂		⋏	⋏	⊓		⋔	⋀	⋏

* Abbreviations as used in 'Creating Original Hand-knitted Lace'
• Possibly first graphical representation for Knitted Lace.
•• System which evolved into modern Burda symbols.

143

Appendix B

❧

Bluebell Baby Set

Figure 170.

In this project the main colour is used as a background to emphasise the lace pattern. The system of tucks and hems also provides a firm edge where they are most useful. This idea lends itself to further exploitation in a variety of projects and in some cases can be used very successfully in conjunction with the double knitting technique described in Chapter 4, Figure 75.

Although the garments have been knitted on sets of two needles the cap and jersey/sweater instructions can easily be adapted to circular knitting. In this case the 3 extra stitches required to begin and end the pattern need not be included and these can be added at the completion of the 3 rows of reverse stocking stitch to keep the stitch numbers and measurements for the rest of the pattern correct.

The pattern and chart of the bluebell design have been fine tuned compared with the chart shown in Chapter 6, Figure 122. The direction of several of the decreases has been changed to give the flower a more rounded shape. Having tried this pattern, the reader may wish to create a version which is a mirror image and perhaps an all over pattern by repeating the pattern several times—perhaps on the diagonal—plotting the position of the bluebells on a chart first. Then, why not a border to match?

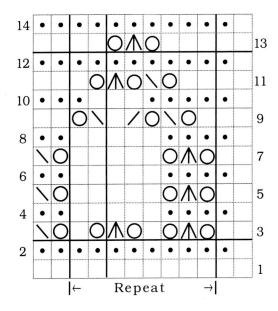

Figure 171. Revised bluebell.

Materials

The original was knitted in Shepherd Baby Wool 3-ply of 120m (132 yds) per 25g ball.

For the complete set with either the cap or the bonnet, 6 balls of the main colour and 1 of the contrast were required. To knit the second hat 1 ball of main colour and extra white will be required.

To knit each item separately. The bonnet, cap and booties require 1 ball each of the main colour and a small quantity of the contrast. For the jersey (sweater) allow 4 balls of the main colour and 1 ball of the contrast.

Needles

One pair each of needles size 2.75mm (UK 12, US 1) and 3mm (UK 11, US 2). One needle size 2mm (UK 14, US 00) for picking up loops for tucks and hems. For jersey/sweater—circular needle size 2.75mm for the yoke, two stitch holders or spare needles and small safety pins. Three small buttons. A slightly larger button for cap.

Measurements

Cap stretches to 48cm (18 3/4ins).
Bonnet measures 30cm (12ins) around face.
Booties foot length 12cm (4.5ins).
Jersey/sweater to fit 48cm (18ins) chest. Sleeve 16cm (6ins).
Length to back of neck 26cm (10ins).

Tension

8 sts and 10 rows to 5cm (2ins) measured over stocking stitch on size 3mm needles.

Abbreviations as given in Appendix A.

Pattern for Bluebell

Multiple of 8 sts plus 3.

Rows 1 and **2.** Knit.
Row 3. K1, * yo, sl 2, k1 p2sso, yo, k1. Repeat from * until 2 sts remain. Yo, k2 tog.
Rows 4, 6 and **8.** K2, * p5, k3. Repeat from * to last st. K1.
Rows 5 and **7.** K1, * yo, sl 2, k1 p2sso, yo, k5. Repeat from * until 2 sts remain. Yo, k2 tog.
Row 9. K2, * yo, ssk, yo, k2 tog, k1, ssk, yo, k1. Repeat from * ending last repeat with k2.
Row 10. K3, * p3, k5. Repeat from * to end.
Row 11. K3, * yo, ssk, yo, sl 2, k1 p2sso, yo, k3. Repeat from * to end.
Rows 12 and **14.** Knit.
Row 13. K4, * yo, sl 1, k2 tog psso, yo, k5. Repeat from * ending last repeat with k4.

Bonnet

With size 2.75mm needles and main colour wool, cast on 83 stitches and work 13 rows in stocking stitch beginning and ending with a knit row.

Wrong side of work is now facing knitter.

Continue by working 5 rows in reverse stocking stitch beginning and ending with a knit row.

With size 2mm needle and on the wrong side of the work, pick up the loops forming the 13th stocking-stitch row.

Change to contrast colour and work first row of Bluebell pattern at the same time knitting together one stitch from each needle to make a tuck.

Complete the Bluebell pattern.

With size 2mm needle pick up loops of cast-on edge. Change to main colour and knit one row, knitting together one stitch from each needle as above to make a hem.

** Work 3 rows in reverse stocking stitch beginning and ending with a knit row. **

(Right side of work now facing knitter.) Continue in stocking stitch for 21 rows.

Repeat from ** to **.

Change to contrast colour and work rows 1 to 8 inclusive of Bluebell pattern.

Row 9. K2 tog, * yo, ssk, yo, k2 tog, k1, ssk, yo, k1. Repeat from * ending last repeat with k2 tog instead of k1.

Row 10. K2, * p3, k5. Repeat from * ending last repeat k4 instead of k5.

Row 11. K2 tog, * yo, ssk, yo, sl 2, k1 p2sso, yo, sl 1, k2 tog psso. Repeat from * to last 7 sts. Yo, ssk, yo, sl 2, k1 p2sso, yo, k2 tog.

Rows 12 and **14.** Knit.

Row 13. K2 tog, * yo, sl 1, k1 psso. Repeat from * to last 2 sts. Yo, k2 tog.

Change to main colour and knit 1 row then repeat from ** to ** once. 42 sts. (Right side facing.) Complete crown as follows:

Row 1. K5, k2 tog to end of row.

Row 2 and all alternate rows. Purl.

Row 3. * K4, k2 tog. Repeat from * to end of row.

Row 5. * K3, k2 tog. Repeat from * to end of row.

Row 7. * K2, k2 tog. Repeat from * to end of row.

Row 9. * K1, k2 tog. Repeat from * to end of row.

Break thread and draw through remaining stitches.

Make a seam from centre of crown to the first row of reverse stocking stitch at the beginning of the last Bluebell repeat. With main colour and size 2.75mm needles and right side of work facing, pick up and knit 2 stitches for every 3 rows from sides of bonnet along neck edge and work 5 rows in reverse stocking stitch. Cast off, fold over towards inside and stitch or graft into place to make a narrow hem. Make two twisted cords threading them through the stitches where the tuck and the neck hem meet before allowing the cord to twist on itself. The bonnet acts as the tensioning weight.

The Cap

With size 2.75 needles and main colour cast on 91 stitches and work as for bonnet until the directions for reverse stocking stitch given between ** to ** have been completed for the first time.

Work 27 rows in stocking stitch decreasing 3 stitches evenly on the last row.

Work three rows in reverse stocking stitch ** to **.

Shape Crown:
Row 1. * K9, k2 tog. Repeat from * to end of row.
Row 2 and **all alternate rows.** Purl.
Row 3. * K8, k2 tog. Repeat from * to end of row.
Row 5. * K7, k2 tog. Repeat from * to end of row.
Row 7. * K6, k2 tog. Repeat from * to end of row.
Rows 9, 11, 13, 15 and **17.** As rows 1, 3, 5, 7 and 9 of bonnet crown.
Break thread and draw through remaining stitches.

Complete by making a seam from crown to lower edge. Stitch edges of lace border separately using matching yarn. Finish crown by knitting a small circle of reverse stocking stitch to cover a small button to be stitched in the centre.

The Booties

With size 2.75mm needles and main colour cast on 47 sts and knit 1 row.

Row 1. K1, incB, k20, incB, k1, incB, k20, incB, k1.
Row 2 and **all alternate rows.** Knit.
Row 3. K1, incB, k22, incB, k1, incB, k22, incB, k1.
Row 5. K1, incB, k24, incB, k1, incB, k24, incB, k1.
Row 7. K1, incB, k26, incB, k1, incB, k26, incB, k1.
Row 9. K1, incB, k28, incB, k1, incB, k28, incB, k1.
Row 10. Knit.
Work 9 rows stocking stitch beginning and ending with a knit row then work 3 rows reverse stocking stitch beginning and ending with a knit row.
Knit 39, k2 tog tbl, turn and work short rows as follows:
Row 1. Sl 1, p11, p2 tog, turn.

Row 2. Sl 1, k11, k2 tog tbl, turn.

Repeat these 2 rows until 44 stitches remain across both needles.

Next row. P27, p2 tog, p15.

Make holes for cord.

* K1, yo, k2 tog. Repeat from * to last stitch. K1.

Purl 1 row and knit 1 row.

Work 3 rows reverse stocking stitch as described above then change to contrast yarn.

Work Bluebell pattern. Change to main colour and work 5 rows of reverse stocking stitch.

Make a tuck as described for bonnet by picking up loops of stitches of last Bluebell pattern row on a size 2mm needle.

Work 12 rows stocking stitch beginning with a purl row.

Graft these stitches to the loops of the stitches of the first row of Bluebell pattern.

Stitch up foot seam and back of leg using matching yarn for each section, stitching Bluebell section separately. Make twisted cords from main colour to thread through holes at ankle.

The Jersey/Sweater

Using size 2.75mm needles and main colour cast on 83 stitches and work as for bonnet until the first 3 rows of reverse stocking stitch ** to ** have been completed.

Change to size 3mm needles and continue in stocking stitch for 40 rows.

Tie markers of contrast thread at each end of last row to indicate armholes.

Work 10 more rows in stocking stitch.***

Back Opening:

Knit 44, turn. Continue on these 44 sts as follows:

Row 1. K5, purl to end.

Row 2. Knit.

Repeat these 2 rows once more and then row 1.

Buttonhole row:

Knit to last 3 sts. Yo, k2 tog, k1.

Repeat rows 1 and 2 four times and then row 1.

Shape for Yoke:

Knit 27, turn. Sl 1, purl to end.

Knit 23, turn. Sl 1, purl to end.

Continue on remaining stitches decreasing one stitch at neck edge every row 4 times and then each alternate row twice. (17 stitches.) Knit 6 rows in stocking stitch.

Place all stitches on to a stitch holder.

Return to 39 unworked sts of back. Join wool at centre and cast on 5 stitches for facing or pick up and knit the five loops at the base of garter stitch facing already worked.

Work as above reversing shaping and omitting button hole.

Front:
Work as for back to ***.

Shape for Yoke:
K36, ssk turn. Sl 1, purl to end.
K30, ssk turn. Sl 1, purl to end.
K24, ssk turn. Sl 1, purl to end.

Continue in stocking stitch decreasing at neck edge every row 4 times, then every alternate row 3 times. (17 stitches.)

Work 16 rows in stocking stitch and then place all stitches on a needle holder.

Return to unworked stitches and rejoin wool. With right side facing knit to end and then work as above reversing shaping.

Yoke:
Graft the 17 shoulder stitches on the fronts to the matching stitches on the back.

With size 2.75mm circular needle, main colour, right side facing and beginning at the centre back, slip the first 5 stitches from the needle holder on to a small safety pin and then knit the rest of the stitches picking up a loop and knitting into the back of it.

Or knit into side of the stitch of row below at the point where the work was turned to prevent a hole from forming.

Where the decreases begin pick up and knit 12 stitches to shoulder and then pick up and knit 27 stitches along front to meet the stitches on stitch holder.

Knit across these stitches making the extra stitches between each group as for the back.

Pick up and knit 27 stitches along other side to shoulder and 12 stitches along back yoke to remaining stitches on stitch holder.

Work these as for other side omitting 5 edge stitches as before. (151 stitches.)

Work from ** to ** as for bonnet once.

Change to contrast colour and work decrease row as follows:

K7, k2 tog, * k3, k2 tog. Repeat from * to last 7 sts. K7. (123 stitches.)

Work rows 1—10 inclusive of Bluebell pattern then continue with decrease rows thus.

Row 11. K3,* yo, ssk, yo, sl 2, k1 p2sso, yo, sl 1, k2 tog psso. Repeat from * to last 8sts. Yo, ssk, sl 2 k1 p2sso, yo, k3.

Rows 12 and **14.** Knit.

Row 13. K4,* yo, sl 1 k2 tog psso. Repeat from * to last 4 sts. Yo, k4. (67 stitches.)

Row 15. Change to main colour and knit 1 row.

Work 7 rows reverse stocking stitch. With size 2mm needle pick up loops of Row 15.

Next row make tuck by knitting stitches from both needles together as before, then purl one row.

Next row. K5, incB,* K1, incB. Repeat from * to last 6 sts. K6.

Next row. Purl.

Next row. K7, * incB, k1, incB, k3. Repeat from * to last 4 sts. K4. (123 stitches.)

Work 8 more rows in stocking stitch. Graft stitches to row of loops at beginning of Bluebell section.

Complete garter stitch borders with size 3mm needles and main colour. Make 2 more buttonholes at regular intervals. Stitch to edge of back opening.

The sleeves:

With main colour and size 2.75mm needles cast on 35 stitches and work as for bonnet until the 3 rows of reverse stocking stitch ** to ** have been completed.

Next row. * IncB, k2. Repeat from * to last 2 stitches. IncB, K1.

Next row. Purl.

Change to needles size 3mm and continue in stocking stitch increasing at beginning and end of 5th and following 8th rows until there are 59 stitches on the needle ending with a purl row. Add extra rows at this stage if a longer sleeve is required.

Work 3 rows reverse stocking stitch. Cast off or, if preferred, graft stitches to armhole opening.

To make up stitch side and sleeve seams matching borders, using matching yarn for each section. Sew seams of Bluebell lace separately. Sew on buttons to match button holes.

Appendix C

'Chainging' Directions

Figure 172.

Tray cloth or Table mat

The size of this cloth can easily be changed to suit the requirements of the knitter and the design is equally suitable for large items like a tablecloth or bedspread.

This project has been included to illustrate the way stitches can be manipulated to achieve effects which would initially appear to be impossible. However in this case, with the exception of the crocheted edging, no implements other than two knitting needles have been used to create the lace design.

Garter stitch has been used as the background as it provides a contrasting texture for the chains of the decreases outlining the openwork areas. As more rows of garter stitch are required for an equivalent length of stocking stitch, this reduced any

Figure 173. Chart for border.

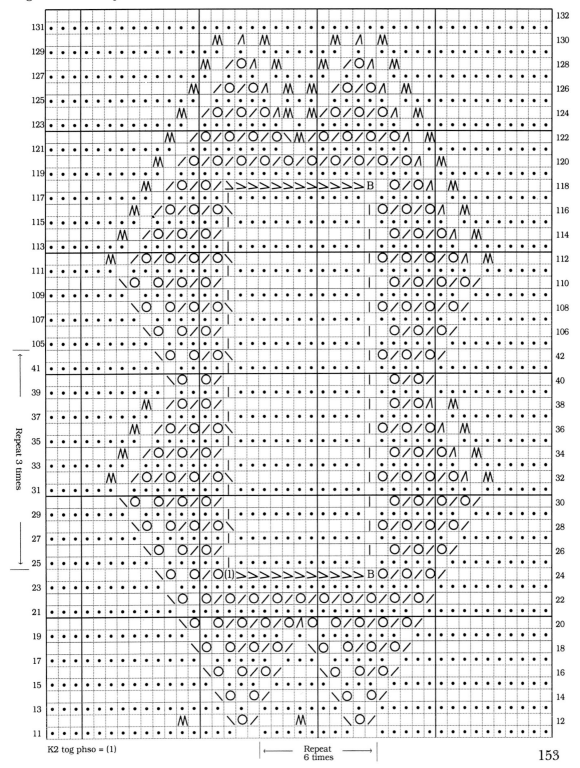

K2 tog phso = (1)

tendency for the background to pucker as the chains moved across at an angle. Slipping the vertical chains on alternate rows allowed them to sit on the surface of the knitting. The method of creating the horizontal chain is described in both *Creative Knitting* (pages 74-75) by Mary Walker Phillips and *The Principles of Knitting* by June Hemmons Hiatt.

This is my first solution for this design and I can already see places where the outline can be sharpened even further. I hope the reader will also consider improvements and use and extend this idea as one with a wide range of possibilities.

Variations could include using the centre for further geometrical shapes, a series of coasters and cushion covers demonstrating variations—perhaps a full size tablecloth in a mercerised cotton with a woven linen centre.

Terms, symbols and abbreviations used are as given in Appendix A. Special abbreviation: phso—pass horizontal stitch over.

Materials

Two 28g (1oz) balls of Strutts No. 5 Lustre Knittings cotton in natural for each mat.

Needles

Size 2.75mm (UK 12, US 2). Crochet hook size 2.75mm (UK 12, US 2).

Measurements

46cm (18ins) wide—34cm (13ins) deep.

Tension

14 sts and 18 rows over 5cm (2ins) of stocking stitch.

Cast on 103 sts and knit 10 rows in garter stitch.

Row 11. K16, * p2, k8. Repeat from * to last 7st. K7.
Row 12. K15, * k2 tog, yo, ssk, k3, m1, k3. Repeat from * to last 8 sts. K8.
Row 13. K15, * p1, k1, p1, k7. Repeat from * to last 8 sts. K8.
Row 14. K14, * k2 tog, yo, k1, yo, ssk, k5. Repeat from * to last 9 sts. K9.
Row 15. K14, * p1, k3, p1, k5. Repeat from * to last 9 sts. K9.
Row 16. K13, * (k2 tog, yo) twice, k1, yo, ssk, k3. Repeat from * to last 10 sts. K10.
Row 17. K13, * p1, k5, p1, k3. Repeat from * to last 10 sts. K10.
Row 18. K12, * (k2 tog, yo) three times, k1, yo, ssk, k1. Repeat from * to last 11 sts. K11.
Row 19. K12, * p1, k7, p1, k1. Repeat from * to last 11 sts. K11.

Row 20. K11, * (k2 tog, yo)four times, k1, yo, sl 1, k1, psso, yo. Repeat from * to last 20 sts. (Yo, k2 tog)three times, k1, yo, k1, yo, ssk, k11.

Row 21. K11, p1, knit to last 12 sts. P1, k11.

Row 22. K10, * k2 tog, yo. Repeat from * to last 13 sts. K1, yo, ssk, k10.

Row 23. K10, p1, knit to last 11 sts. P1, k10.

Row 24. K9, (k2 tog, yo)three times, incB, work horizontal stitch (hs) with increased stitch as described in Appendix A until 16 sts remain. K2 tog, phso, yo, k2 tog, yo, k1, yo, ssk, k9.

Row 25. K9, p1, k5, sl 1 wyif, knit until 16 sts remain. P1, k5, p1, k9.

Row 26. K8, (k2 tog, yo)three times, k1, sl 1 wyib, knit until 15 sts remain. (K2 tog, yo)twice, k1, yo, ssk, k8.

Row 27. K8, p1, k6, sl 1 wyif, knit until 16 sts remain. P1, k6, p1, k8.

Row 28. K7, (k2 tog, yo)four times, sl 1 wyib, knit until 16 sts remain. Ssk, (yo, k2 tog)twice, yo, k1, yo, ssk, k7.

Row 29. K7, p1, k7, sl 1 wyif, knit until 16 sts remain. P1, k7, p1, k7.

Row 30. K6, (k2 tog, yo)four times, k1, sl 1 wyib, knit until 15 sts remain. (K2 tog, yo)three times, k1, yo, ssk, k6.

Row 31. K6, p1, k8, sl 1 wyif, knit until 16 sts remain. P1, k8, p1, k6.

Row 32. K5, m1, k1, sl 1, k2 tog, psso, (yo, k2 tog)three times, yo, sl 1, wyib, knit until 16 sts remain. Ssk, (yo, k2 tog)four times, k1, m1, k5.

Row 33. K7, p1, k7, sl 1 wyif, knit until 16 stitches remain. P1, k7, p1, k7.

Row 34. K6, m1, k1, sl 1, k2 tog psso, (yo, k2 tog)twice, yo, k1, sl 1 wyib, knit until 15 sts remain. (K2 tog, yo)three times, k2 tog, k1, m1, k6.

Row 35. K8, p1, k6, sl 1 wyif, knit until 16 sts remain. P1, k6, p1, k8.

Row 36. K7, m1, k1, sl 1, k2 tog psso, (yo, k2 tog)twice, yo, sl 1 wyib, knit until 16 sts remain. Ssk, (yo, k2 tog)three times, k1, m1, k7.

Row 37. K9, p1, k5, sl 1 wyif, knit until 16 sts remain. P1, k5, p1, k9.

Row 38. K8, m1, k1, sl 1, k2 tog psso, yo, k2 tog, yo, k1, sl 1 wyib, knit until 15 sts remain. (K2 tog, yo)twice, k2 tog, k1, m1, k8.

Row 39. K10, p1, k4, sl 1 wyif, knit until 16 sts remain, p1, k4, p1, k10.

Row 40. K10, (k2 tog, yo)twice, k1, sl 1 wyib, knit until 15 sts remain. K2 tog, yo, k1, yo, ssk, k10.

Row 41. K10, p1, k4, sl 1 wyif, knit until 16 sts remain. P1, k4, p1, k10.

Row 42. K9, (k2 tog, yo)three times, sl 1 wyib, knit until 16 sts remain. Ssk, yo, k2 tog, yo, k1, yo, ssk, k9.

Repeat rows 25 to 42 inclusive three times more and then rows 25 to 37 inclusive once.

Complete design in the following manner.

Row 1. K8, m1, k1, sl 1, k2 tog psso, yo, k2 tog, yo, k1, incB, work horizontal stitch as above until 16 sts remain. K1, phso, (k2 tog, yo)twice, k2 tog, k1, m1, k8.

Row 2. K10, p1, knit until 11 sts remain. P1, k10.

Row 3. K9, m1, k1, sl 1, k2 tog psso, * yo, k2 tog. Repeat from * to last 10 sts. K1, m1, k9.

Row 4. K11, p1, knit until 12 sts remain. P1, k11.

Row 5. K10, m1, k1, sl 1, k2 tog psso, * (yo, k2 tog)four times, m1, ssk. Repeat from * to last 20 sts. (Yo, k2 tog)four times, k1, m1, k10.

Row 6. K12, * p1, k7, p1, k1. Repeat from * to last 11 sts. K11.

Row 7. K11, m1, k1, * sl 1, k2 tog psso, (yo, k2 tog)three times, m1, k1, m1. Repeat from * to last 21 sts. Sl 1, k2 tog psso, (yo, k2 tog)three times, k1, m1, k 11.

Row 8. K13, * p1, k5, p1, k3. Repeat from * to last 10 sts. K10.

Row 9. K12, m1, k1, * sl 1, k2 tog psso, (yo, k2 tog)twice, (k1, m1)twice, k1. Repeat from * to last 20 sts. Sl 1, k2 tog psso, (yo, k2 tog)twice, k1, m1, k 12.

Row 10. K14, * p1, k3, p1, k5. Repeat from * until last 9 sts. K9.

Row 11. K13, * m1, k1, sl 1, k2 tog psso, yo, k2 tog, k1, m1, k3. Repeat from * to last 10 sts. K10.

Row 12. K15, * p1, k1, p1, k7. Repeat from * to last 8 sts. K8.

Row 13. K14, * m1, k1, sl 1, k2 tog psso, k1, m1, k5. Repeat from * to last 9 sts. K9.

Row 14. Knit.

Work 10 rows in garter stitch and then cast off.

With crochet hook work 1 row of double crochet (US single crochet) along each side working one stitch in each stitch of cast-on and cast-off edges. Along sides work one stitch for every 2 rows. Work a second round using the same stitch but working in the opposite direction—ie from left to right—to give a raised, twisted edge called Crab Stitch. Fasten off.

Appendix D

❧

Curtain worked in Rosebud and Leaf pattern

Edward Field

Figure 174. Detail of rosebud curtain.

This pattern uses the rosebud motif featured on the cover. The development of the motif is described in Chapter 7. It also illustrates a very useful method of construction, as well as taking advantage of the techniques discussed in Chapter 4 where considerable areas are knitted in 'lace' formed by using large sized needles in relation to the grist of the yarn.

The curtain has been constructed in panels of open mesh areas separated by panels featuring the rosebud pattern which is worked on finer needles to give definition to the motif. This construction allows for considerable variation in size and shape, so the knitter should find it relatively easy to adapt the pattern to suit any window size or shape. The technique for joining the strips can also be easily adapted to other situations where the knitter wishes to avoid sewing seams.

By using patterns with a more solid fabric for the plain area between the decorative strips, this construction lends itself well to making such items as afghans, screens, cushion covers and even some garment shapes. The width of the strips is entirely up to the designer. The only critical factor is to ensure that the different needle sizes, in combination with the number of stitches picked up each side of the strips to be joined, ensure a flat fabric when the piece is finished.

The curtain in the pattern has been designed to fit a window measuring 97cm (38ins) high and 92cm (36ins) wide, as shown in Figure 22, page 29. The two side strips have been joined by a shaped piece to frame the view from the window. However, just as the length of the curtain can be adjusted, so also can the width, and the shaped piece can be deleted altogether if desired.

As the curtain was knitted in crochet cotton, the holes at each edge of the mesh strips have become larger than I had planned, to counter this, the instructions substitute the 'yarn over' used in the original with 'make one' to give a firmer and more controlled hole size. A border of two stitches in garter stitch would be just as suitable and make a more stable edge.

Terms, symbols and abbreviations see Appendix A.

Materials

4 50g (385m) balls of DMC crochet cotton.

Needles

Size 4mm (UK 8, US 6), 2.75mm (UK 12, US 2) and 2mm (UK 14, US 0). One stitch holder and four large safety pins. Crochet hook size 2.75mm (UK 12, US 2).

Tension

To measure 20 sts and 26 rows over 5 cm (2ins) worked in stocking stitch on size 2mm needles.

Rosebud and Leaf Pattern

Row 1. Ssk, yo, k2, k2 tog, yo, k3, yo, ssk, k2 tog, yo, k1, yo, ssk, k2 tog, yo, k3, yo, ssk, k2, yo, sl 2, k1, p2sso.

Row 2. P1, k4, p5, k7, p5, k4, p2 tog.

Row 3. Ssk, k1, k2 tog, yo, k1, m1, k2 tog, m1, k1, yo, ssk, k2 tog, yo, k1, yo, ssk, k2 tog, yo, k1, m1, ssk, m1, k1, yo, ssk, k1, sl 2, k1, p2sso.

Row 4. P1, k2, p7, k7, p7, k2, p2 tog.

Row 5. Ssk, k1, yo, k2, k2 tog, m1, k1, ssk, yo, k2 tog, yo, k3, yo, ssk, yo, k2 tog, k1, m1, ssk, k2, yo, k1, sl 2, k1 p2sso.

Row 6. P1, k1, p8, k7, p8, k1, p2 tog.

Row 7. Ssk, yo, k2, k2 tog, m1, k1, ssk, yo, k2 tog, yo, k1, yo, sl 2, k1, p2sso, yo, k1, yo, ssk, yo, k2 tog, k1, m1, ssk, k2, yo, sl 2, k1, p2sso.

Row 8. P9, k4, p1, k4, p8, p2 tog.

Row 9. Ssk, yo, k1, k2 tog, m1, k1, ssk, yo, k2 tog, yo, k2, yo, sl 2, k1, p2sso, yo, k2, yo, ssk, yo, k2 tog, k1, m1, ssk, k1, yo, sl 2, k1, p2sso.

Row 10. P8, k5, p1, k5, p7, p2 tog.

Row 11. Ssk, yo, k2 tog, m1, k1, ssk, yo, k2 tog, yo, k3, yo, sl 2, k1, p2sso, yo, k3, yo, ssk, yo, k2 tog, k1, m1, ssk, yo, sl 2, k1, p2sso.

Row 12. P7, k6, p1, k6, p6, p2 tog.

Row 13. Ssk, yo, k2 tog, m1, ssk, yo, k2 tog, yo, k2, k2 tog, yo, sl 2, (k1, p1, k1) in next stitch (called inc3), p2sso 3inc sts, yo, ssk, k2, yo, ssk, yo, k2 tog, m1, ssk, yo, sl 2, k1, p2sso.

Row 14. P6, k6, p3, k6, p5, p2 tog.

Row 15. Ssk, yo, k1, ssk, yo, k2 tog, yo, k4, yo, k2 tog, k1, ssk, yo, k4, yo, ssk, yo, k2 tog, k1, yo, sl 2, k1, p2sso.

Row 16. P5, k7, p3 tog, k7, p4, p2 tog. (2 sts less)

Row 17. (Ssk, yo)twice, k2 tog, yo, k3, k2 tog, yo, sl 2, inc 3, p2sso 3 inc sts, yo, ssk, k3, yo, ssk, yo, k2 tog, yo, sl 2, k1, p2sso.

Row 18. P1, k10, (p1, yo)twice, p1, k10, p2 tog.

Row 19. K1, (k2 tog, yo)twice, k3, k2 tog, yo, incB in 2 sts tog, yo, k1 B, k1, k1 B, yo, incB in 2 sts tog, yo, ssk, k3, (yo, ssk)twice, k2 tog, (2 sts gained).

Row 20. P1, k9, p2, k1, p3, k1, p2, k9, p2 tog.

Row 21. K1, yo, ssk, k2 tog, yo, k2, k2 tog, yo, sl 2, k1, p2sso, yo, k2 tog, m1, k1, m1, ssk, yo, sl 2, k1, p2sso, yo, ssk, k2, yo, ssk, k2 tog, yo, k2 tog. (2 sts less).

Row 22. P1, k8, p1, k1, p5, k1, p1, k8, p2 tog.

Row 23. K1, yo, ssk, k2, yo, k2 tog, k1, yo, k2 tog, yo, k2 tog, m1, k3, ssk, yo, ssk, yo, k1, ssk, yo, k2, k2 tog, yo, k2 tog.

Row 24. P2, k7, p1, k1, p6, k1, p1, k7, p1, p2 tog.

Row 25. Ssk, m1, yo, ssk, k1, yo, k2 tog, k1, k2 tog, k1, yo, k1, ssk, k2 tog, k1, yo, k1, ssk, k1, ssk, yo, k1, k2 tog, yo, m1, sl 2, k1, p2sso.

Row 26. P3, k8, p4, k8, p2, p2 tog.

Row 27. Ssk, m1, k1, yo, ssk, k1, yo, k2 tog, k3, yo, sl 1, k3, psso 3 sts, yo, k3, ssk, yo, k1, k2 tog, yo, k1, m1, sl 2, k1, p2sso.

Row 28. P4, k8, p3, k8, p3, p2 tog.

Row 29. Ssk, m1, k2, yo, ssk, k1, yo, k2 tog, k1, k2 tog, yo, k2 tog, k1, yo, ssk, k1, ssk, yo, k1, k2 tog, yo, k2, m1, sl 2, k1, p2sso.

Row 30. P5, k7, k into next 2 sts tog, then once into first st and once into second st to make 3 sts, k7, p4, p2 tog.

Row 31. Ssk, m1, k3, yo, ssk, k1, yo, k2 tog, k7, ssk, yo, k1, k2 tog, yo, k3, m1, sl 2, k1, p2sso.

Row 32. P6, k15, p5, p2 tog.

Row 33. Ssk, k3, yo, k1, yo, ssk, k1, yo, k2 tog, k5, ssk, yo, k1, k2 tog, yo, k1, yo, k3, sl 2, k1, p2sso.

Row 34. P5, k17, p4, p2 tog.

Row 35. Ssk, k2, yo, k3, yo, ssk, k1, yo, k2 tog, k3, ssk, yo, k1, k2 tog, yo, k3, yo, k2, sl 2, k1, p2sso.

Row 36. P4, k19, p3, p2 tog.

Row 37. Ssk, k1, yo, k2, k2 tog, yo, k1, yo, ssk, k1, yo, k2 tog, k1, ssk, yo, k1, k2 tog, yo, k1, yo, ssk, k2, yo, k1, sl 2, k1, p2sso.

Row 38. P3, k3, p3, k9, p3, k3, p2, p2 tog.

Begin by making two side strips in the Lace Background Stitch which has been attributed to Dorothy Reade of Eugene, Oregon, USA.

Cast on 29 stitches loosely and knit one row.

Row 1. (Right side). K3, * yo, sl 1, k1, yo, psso the k1 and the yo *. Repeat from * to * to last 2 sts. M1, k2 tog or k2.

Row 2. K2, * p2, dr 1 (drop yo of previous row) *. Repeat from * to * to last 3 sts. P1, m1, k2 tog or p1, k2.

Row 3. K2, * yo, sl 1, k1, yo, psso the k1 and the yo *. Repeat from * to * to last 3 sts. K1, m1, k2 tog or k3.

Row 4. K2, p1, * dr 1 (drop yo of previous row), p2 *. Repeat from * to * to last 2 sts. M1, k2 tog or k2.

For each repeat of the rosebud motif, 19 rows of the Lace Background are required. For the side strips there were 10 repeats of the rosebud, therefore 190 rows are required. Place stitches on large safety pin and make second strip in the same manner.

Using a size 2mm needle and beginning at the top of the first strip with the right side facing, pick up one loop for each row along the side to the cast-on edge. Using a second 2mm needle and beginning at the top of the second strip but with wrong side facing, pick up a loop for each row along the side to the cast-on edge.

With the wrong sides facing, join in the cotton and cast 27 stitches loosely on to the left-hand side strip. Knit 27 then turn. Begin knitting Rosebud Pattern, noting that the last instruction for each row includes one of the picked up stitches. Working the 38 rows of the pattern 10 times will work off all the stitches from each needle. Place all remaining stitches (including those on the safety pins) on to a stitch holder.

Repeat this for the second side.

Using the same technique, make two short strips of the Lace Background Pattern of 58 rows each and join as above with three repeats of the rosebud pattern after picking up 57 stitches along each side piece.

Now make the shaped Lace Background pieces as follows, but reverse the shaping for the second piece by working increases at opposite edge. These increases have been made by inserting a 'm1' at the shaped edge and this instruction has been underlined in the pattern. It will be noted that in the section where the Background Lace is introduced, each row ends with 'm1, k2 tog.' This can be replaced with 'k2' if desired.

Cast on 2 sts on size 4mm (UK 8, US 6).

Rows 1 and **following alternate rows**
to and including **row 33**. Knit.

Row 2. K1, <u>m1</u>, k1.
Rows 4 and **6.** K1, m1, k2 tog.
Row 8. K1, <u>m1</u>, k2.
Rows 10, 12 and **14.** K2, m1, k2 tog.
Row 16. K1, <u>m1</u>, k1, m1, k2 tog.
Rows 18, 20 and **22.** K3, m1, k2 tog.
Row 24. K1, <u>m1</u>, k2, m1, k2 tog.
Rows 26 and **28.** K4, m1, k2 tog.
Row 30. K3, <u>m1</u>, k1, m1, k2 tog.
Row 32. K5, m1, k2 tog.
Row 34. K3, <u>m1</u>, k2, m1, k2 tog.

Introduce Lace Background Stitch.

Row 1. (right side facing knitter) K3, yo, sl 1, k1, yo, psso, k1, m1, k2 tog.
Row 2. K3, p2, dr 1, <u>m1</u>, k1, m1, k2 tog.
Row 3. K3, yo, sl 1, k1, yo, psso, k2, m1, k2 tog.
Row 4. K3, <u>m1</u>, p3, dr 1, k1, m1, k2 tog.
Row 5. K4, yo, sl 1, k1, yo, psso, k2, m1, k2 tog.
Row 6. K3, <u>m1</u>, p3, dr 1, k2, m1, k2 tog.
Row 7. K3, (yo, sl 1, k1, yo, psso)twice, k2, m1, k2 tog.
Row 8. K3, <u>m1</u>, p1, (p2, dr 1)twice, k1, m1, k2 tog.
Row 9. K4, (yo, sl 1, k1, yo, psso)twice, k1, m1, k1, <u>m1</u>, k2 tog.
Row 10. K3, <u>m1</u>, p4, dr 1, p2, dr 1, k2, m1, k2 tog.
Row 11. K3, (yo, sl 1, k1, yo, psso)4 times, <u>m1</u>, k1, m1, k2 tog.

161

Row 12. K3, <u>m1</u>, p3, dr 1, (p2, dr 1)twice, k1, m1, k2 tog.

Row 13. K4, (yo, sl 1, k1, yo, psso)four times, k1, <u>m1</u>, k1, m1, k2 tog.

Row 14. K3, <u>m1</u>, p4, dr 1, (p2, dr 1)three times, k2, m1, k2 tog.

Row 15. K3, (yo, sl 1, k1, yo, psso)six times, <u>m1</u>, k1, m1, k2 tog.

Row 16. K3, <u>m1</u>, p3, dr 1, (p2, dr 1)five times, k1, m1, k2 tog.

Row 17. K4, (yo, sl 1, k1, yo, psso)six times, k1, <u>m1</u>, k1, m1, k2 tog.

Row 18. K3, <u>m1</u>, p4, dr 1, (p2, dr 1)five times, k2, m1, k2 tog.

Row 19. K3, (yo, sl 1, k1, yo, psso)eight times, <u>m1</u>, k1, m1, k2 tog.

Row 20. K3, <u>m1</u>, p3, dr 1, (p2, dr 1)seven times, k1, m1, k2 tog.

Row 21. K4, (yo, sl 1, k1, yo, psso)eight times, k1, <u>m1</u>, k1, m1, k2 tog.

Row 22. K3, <u>m1</u>, p4, dr 1, (p2, dr 1)seven times, K2, m1, k2 tog.

Row 23. K3, (yo, sl 1, k1, yo, psso)ten times, <u>m1</u>, k1, m1, k2 tog.

Row 24. K3, p3, dr 1, (p2, dr 1)nine times, k1, m1, k2 tog. (27 sts.)

Continue on these 27 stitches in Background Lace stitch for a further 58 rows and then place stitches on safety pin.

To join these pieces to the side sections already made, pick up 115 stitches along the longer straight side, ready to be worked on to the edge of the rosebud section as soon as there are only six more rosebud repeats to be worked to complete the length of the section. In the meantime, work the rosebud repeat four times along the edge of the curtain to which the shaped piece is to be attached after picking up 190 stitches from the top to the lower edge, as described above.

To make the edge of the curtain firmer, three extra stitches were added and knitted in garter stitch until the shaped piece was joined in. At this point the three stitches were put on a safety pin and later picked up and knitted on to the edge of the curtain using the 2mm needles. These stitches were grafted to the three matching stitches being held on the other side.

Figure 175a shows how the rosebud motif at the lower edge was adapted to shape the curtain for a gathered edge.

The shorter edge of the shaped piece is joined to the centre section by picking up the stitches from top to lower edge, to be joined by three repeats of the rosebud motif.

When all sections are joined, then transfer the stitches being held on safety pins and/or stitch holders on to size 2.75mm needles (UK 12, US 2). Make a casing by working in stocking stitch to the depth required for one half of the casing and then work one row in reverse stocking stitch to define the fold, followed by stocking stitch to complete the other side of the casing. Cast off loosely and stitch firmly into place. Complete the lower edges the same way, making a button hole in the centre of the casing on the right side through which a cord or ribbon can be drawn. As a final finishing, a three-chain picot edge was crocheted along the edge of the curtain and along the reverse stocking stitch row of the casings. A twisted cord of the crochet cotton was made to draw in the lower edge. One end of each cord was attached to the outer edges of the casing and then threaded through the button hole and tied.

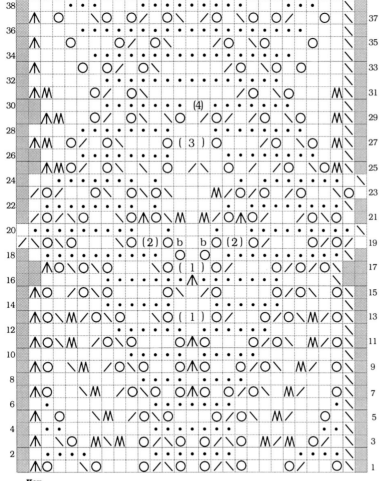

Figure 175. Rosebud chart.

Key

(1) = Slip 2, (k1, p1, k1), into next st. Pass 2 slip sts over 3 increases sts.

(2) = IncB into 2 sts together.

(3) = Slip 1, k3, pass slipped st over 3 sts.

(4) = Knit into 2 sts tog then once into first st then once into second st (3 sts)

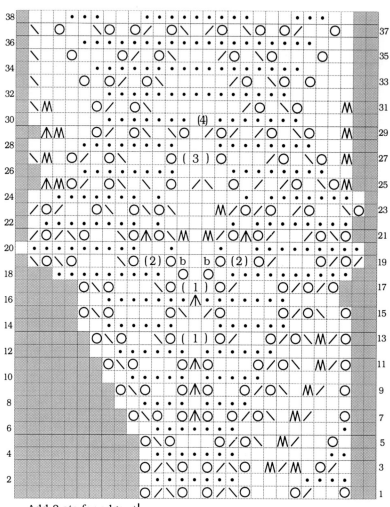

*Figure 175a. Rosebud
chart - shaped corner.*

Add 3 sts for edge →|

Appendix E

ॐ

Flowering Eucalyptus Shawl

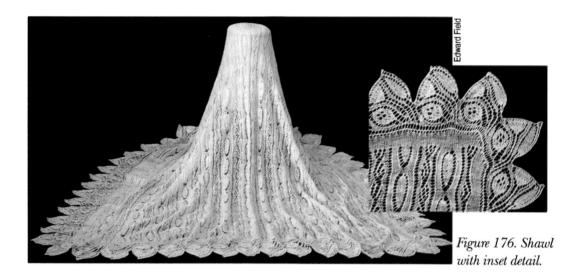

Figure 176. Shawl
with inset detail.

Materials

Yarn 3000 metres (3250 yards) of fine 2-ply baby wool 160 metres
(175 yards) per 28g (1oz). Needles size 3.25mm (UK 10, US 3)

Tension

14 sts and 20 rows to measure 5cm (2ins) over stocking stitch
on size 3.25 needles.

Measurements

148cm (58inches) square.

Eucalyptus Leaf and Bark pattern for centre

Multiples of 47 sts plus 29 sts.

Row 1. K1, (ssk, yo,) twice, ssk, k2,* yo, k2 tog, k8, ssk, yo, k9,
p6, k2, m1, p1, k2, p6, k1, (ssk, yo,)twice, ssk, k2 *. Repeat from
* to * to last 21 sts. Yo, k2 tog, k8, ssk, yo, k9.
Row 2. K1, (ssk, yo,)twice, ssk, k2, p12,* k8, yo, k2 tog, k2, ssk,
yo, p2, k1, p3, yo, k2 tog, k2, ssk, yo, k1, (k2 tog, yo,)twice, k2
tog, k2, p12 *. Repeat from * to * to last 8 sts. K8.

Row 3. K1, (ssk, yo,) twice, ssk, k1, * yo, k2 tog, k8, ssk, yo, k8, p6, k3, p1, k2, p6, k1, (ssk, yo,) twice, ssk, k1 *. Repeat from * to * to last 20 sts. Yo, k2 tog, k8, ssk, yo, k8.

Row 4. K1, (ssk, yo) twice, ssk, k1, p12, * k7, yo, k2 tog, k2, ssk, yo, p2, k1, p3, yo, k2 tog, k2, ssk, yo, k1, (ssk, yo,) twice, ssk, k1, p12 *. Repeat from * to * to last 7 sts. K7.

Row 5. K1, ssk, yo, ssk, k2, * yo, k2 tog, k2, ssk, yo, m3 by working k1, p1, k1, through back of lifted thread between stitches, yo, k2 tog, k2, ssk, yo, k7, p6, k3, p1, k2, p6, k1, ssk, yo, ssk, k2 *. Repeat from * to * to last 19 sts. Yo, k2 tog, k2, ssk, yo, m3, yo, k2 tog, k2, ssk, yo, k7.

Row 6. K1, ssk, yo, ssk, k2, p6, k1, p1, k1, p6, *k6 yo, k2 tog, k2, ssk, yo, p2, k1, p3, yo, k2 tog, k2, ssk, yo, k1, ssk, yo, ssk, k2, p6, k1, p1, k1, p6 *. Repeat from * to * to last 6 sts. K6.

Row 7. K1, ssk, yo, ssk, k1, * yo, k2 tog, k2, ssk, yo, p1, k1, p1, yo, k2 tog, k2, ssk, yo, k6, p6, k3, p1, k2, p6, k1, ssk, yo, ssk, k1 *. Repeat from * to * to last 21 sts. Yo, k2 tog, k2, ssk, yo, p1, k1, p1, yo, k2 tog, k2, ssk, yo, k6.

Row 8. K1, ssk, yo, ssk, k1, p6, k1, p1, k1, p6, * k5, yo, k2 tog, k2, ssk, yo, p2, k1, p3, yo, k2 tog, k2, ssk, yo, k1, ssk, yo, ssk, k1, p6, k1, p1, k1, p6 *. Repeat from * to * to last 5 sts. K5.

Row 9. K1, ssk, yo, k2, * yo, k2 tog, k2, ssk, yo, p1, k1, p1, yo, k2 tog, k2, ssk, yo, k5, p6, k3, p1, k2, p6, k1, k2 tog, yo, k2 *. Repeat from * to * to last 20 sts. Yo, k2 tog, k2, ssk, yo, p1, k1, p1, yo, k2 tog, k2, ssk, yo, k5.

Row 10. K1, ssk, yo, k2, p6, k1, m1, p1, m1, k1, p6,* k5, yo, k2 tog, k2, ssk, yo, p2, k1, p3, yo, k2 tog, k2, ssk, yo, k1, k2 tog, yo, k2, p6, k1, m1, p1, m1, k1, p6 *. Repeat from * to * to last 5 sts. K5.

Row 11. K1, ssk, yo, k2, * yo, k2 tog, k2, ssk, yo, p2, k1, p2, yo, k2 tog, k2, ssk, yo, k5, p6, sl 2, k1, p2sso, p1, k2 tog, p6, k2, yo, k1, yo, k2 *. Repeat from * to * to last 22 sts. Yo, k2 tog, k2, ssk, yo, p2, k1, p2, yo, k2 tog, k2, ssk, yo, k5.

Row 12. K1, ssk, yo, k2, p6, k2, p1, k2, p6, * k7, yo, k2 tog, k2, ssk, yo, sl 2, k1, p2sso, yo, k2 tog, k2, ssk, yo, k2, yo, k1, yo, k2, p6, k2, p1, k2, p6 *. Repeat from * to * to last 5 sts. K5.

Row 13. K1, ssk, yo, k2, * yo, k2 tog, k2, ssk, yo, p2, k1, p2, yo, k2 tog, k2, ssk, yo, k7, p5, p2 tog, p6, k2, yo, k1, yo, k2 tog, yo, k2 *. Repeat from * to * to last 22 sts. Yo, k2 tog, k2, ssk, yo, p2, k1, p2, yo, k2 tog, k2, ssk, yo, k5.

Row 14. K1, ssk, yo, k2, p6, k2, p1, k2, p6, * k9, yo, k2 tog, k8, ssk, yo, k2, yo, k1, yo, k2 tog, yo, k2, p6, k2, p1, k2, p6 *. Repeat from * to * to last 5 sts. K5.

Row 15. K1, ssk, yo, k2, * yo, k2 tog, k2, ssk, yo, p2, k1, p2, yo, k2 tog, k2, ssk, yo, k9, p12, k1, (k2 tog, yo,) three times, k2 *. Repeat from * to * to last 22 sts. Yo, k2 tog, k2, ssk, yo, p2, k1, p2, yo, k2 tog, k2, ssk, yo, k5.

Row 16. K1, ssk, yo, k2, p6, k2, p1, m1, k2, p6, * k9, yo, k2 tog, k8, ssk, yo, k1, (ssk, yo,) three times, k2, p6, k2, p1, m1, k2, p6 *. Repeat from * to * to last 5 sts. K5.

Row 17. K1, ssk, yo, k2, * yo, k2 tog, k2, ssk, yo, p3, k1, p2, yo, k2 tog, k2, ssk, yo, k9, p12, k2, (k2 tog, yo,) twice, k2 tog, k1 *. Repeat from * to * to last 23 sts. Yo, k2 tog, k2, ssk, yo, p3, k1, p2, yo, k2 tog, k2, ssk, yo, k5.

Row 18. K1, ssk, yo, k2, p6, k2, p1, k3, p6, * k8, yo, k2 tog, k8, ssk, yo, k2, (k2 tog, yo,) twice, k2 tog, k1, p6, k2, p1, k3, p6 *. Repeat from * to * to last 5sts. K5.

Row 19. K1, ssk, yo, k2, * yo, k2 tog, k2, ssk, yo, p3, k1, p2, yo, k2 tog, k2, ssk, yo, k8, p12, k1, (k2 tog, yo,) twice, k2 tog, k1 *. Repeat from * to * to last 23 sts. Yo, k2 tog, k2, ssk, yo, p3, k1, p2, yo, k2 tog, k2, ssk, yo, k5.

Row 20. K1, ssk, yo, k2, p6, k2, p1, k3, p6, * k7, yo, k2 tog, k2, ssk, yo, m3, yo, k2 tog, k2, ssk, yo, k1, (k2 tog, yo,) twice, k2 tog, k1, p6, k2, p1, k3, p6 *. Repeat from * to * to last 5 sts. K5.

Row 21. K1, ssk, yo, k2, * yo, k2 tog, k2, ssk, yo, p3, k1, p2, yo, k2 tog, k2, ssk, yo, k7, p6, k1, p1, k1, p6, k2, k2 tog, yo, k2 tog, k1 *. Repeat from * to * to last 23 sts. Yo, k2 tog, k2, ssk, yo, p3, k1, p2, yo, k2 tog, k2, ssk, yo, k5.

Row 22. K1, ssk, yo, k2, p6, k2, p1, k3, p6, * k6, yo, k2 tog, k2, ssk, yo, p1, k1, p1, yo, k2 tog, k2, ssk, yo, k2, k2 tog, yo, k2 tog, k1, p6, k2, p1, k3, p6 *. Repeat from * to * to last 5 sts. K5.

Row 23. K1, ssk, yo, k2, * yo, k2 tog, k2, ssk, yo, p3, k1, p2, yo, k2 tog, k2, ssk, yo, k6, p6, k1, p1, k1, p6, k1, k2 tog, yo, k2 tog, k1 *. Repeat from * to * to last 23 sts. Yo, k2 tog, k2, ssk, yo, p3, k1, p2, yo, k2 tog, k2, ssk, yo, k5.

Row 24. K1, ssk, yo, k2, p6, k2, p1, k3, p6, * k5, yo, k2 tog, k2, ssk, yo, p1, k1, p1, yo, k2 tog, k2, ssk, yo, k1, k2 tog, yo, k2 tog, k1, p6, k2, p1, k3, p6 *. Repeat from * to * to last 5 sts. K5.

Row 25. K1, ssk, yo, k2, * yo, k2 tog, k2, ssk, yo, p3, k1, p2, yo, k2 tog, k2, ssk, yo, k5, p6, k1, m1, p1, m1, k1, p6, k2, yo, ssk, k1 *. Repeat from * to * to last 23 sts. Yo, k2 tog, k2, ssk, yo, p3, k1, p2, yo, k2 tog, k2, ssk, yo, k5.

Row 26. K2, yo, k1, yo, k2, p6, ssk, p1, sl 2, k1, p2sso, p6, * k5, yo, k2 tog, k2, ssk, yo, p2, k1, p2, yo, k2 tog, k2, ssk, yo, k2, yo, k1, yo, k2, p6, ssk, p1, sl 2, k1, p2sso, p6 *. Repeat from * to * to last 5 sts. K5.

Row 27. K2, yo, k1, yo, k2, * yo, k2 tog, k2, ssk, yo, sl 2, k1, p2sso, yo, k2 tog, k2, ssk, yo, k7, p6, k2, p1, k2, p6, k2, yo, k1, yo, k2 *. Repeat from * to * to last 22 sts. Yo, k2 tog, k2, ssk, yo, sl 2, k1, p2sso, yo, k2 tog, k2, ssk, yo, k7.

Row 28. K2, yo, ssk, yo, k1, yo, k2, p6, p2 tog, p5, * k7, yo, k2 tog, k2, ssk, yo, p2, k1, p2, yo, k2 tog, k2, ssk, yo, k2, yo, ssk, yo, k1, yo, k2, p6, p2 tog, p5 *. Repeat from * to * to last 7 sts. K7.

Row 29. K2, yo, ssk, yo, k1, yo, k2, * yo, k2 tog, k8, ssk, yo, k9, p6, k2, p1, k2, p6, k2, yo, ssk, yo, k1, yo, k2 *. Repeat from * to * to last 21 sts. Yo, k2 tog, k8, ssk, yo, k9.

Row 30. K2, (yo, ssk,) three times, k1, p12, * k9, yo, k2 tog, k2, ssk, yo, p2, k1, p2, yo, k2 tog, k2, ssk, yo, k2, (yo, ssk,) three times, k1, p12 *. Repeat from * to * to last 9 sts. K9.

Row 31. K2, (yo, ssk,) three times, k1, * yo, k2 tog, k8, ssk, yo, k9, p6, k2, p1, m1, k2, p6, k2, (yo, ssk,) three times, k1 *. Repeat from * to * to last 21 sts. Yo, k2 tog, k8, ssk, yo, k9.

Row 32. K1, (ssk, yo,) twice, ssk, k2, p12, * k9, yo, k2 tog, k2, ssk, yo, p3, k1, p2, yo, k2 tog, k2, ssk, yo, k1, (ssk, yo,) twice, ssk, k2, p12 *. Repeat from * to * to last 9 sts. K9.

Row 33. K1, (ssk, yo,) twice, ssk, k2, * yo, k2 tog, k8, ssk, yo, k8, p6, k2, p1, k3, p6, k1, (ssk, yo,) twice, ssk, k2 *. Repeat from * to * to last 20 sts. Yo, k2 tog, k8, ssk, yo, k8.

Row 34. K1, (ssk, yo,) twice, ssk, k1, p12, * k8, yo, k2 tog, k2, ssk, yo, p3, k1, p2, yo, k2 tog, k2, ssk, yo, k1, (ssk, yo,) twice, ssk, k1, p12 *. Repeat from * to * to last 8 sts. K8.

Row 35. K1, (ssk, yo,) twice, ssk, k1, * yo, k2 tog, k2, ssk, yo, m3, yo, k2 tog, k2, ssk, yo, k7, p6, k2, p1, k3, p6, k1, (ssk, yo,) twice, ssk, k1 *. Repeat from * to * to last 19 sts. Yo, k2 tog, k2, ssk, yo, m3, yo, k2 tog, k2, ssk, yo, k7.

Row 36. K1, ssk, yo, ssk, k2, p6, k1, p1, k1, p6, * k7, yo, k2 tog, k2, ssk, yo, p3, k1, p2, yo, k2 tog, k2, ssk, yo, k1, ssk, yo, ssk, k2, p6, k1, p1, k1, p6 *. Repeat from * to * to last 7 sts. K7.

Row 37. K1, ssk, yo, ssk, k2, * yo, k2 tog, k2, ssk, yo, p1, k1, p1, yo, k2 tog, k2, ssk, yo, k6, p6, k2, p1, k3, p6, k1, ssk, yo, ssk, k2 *. Repeat from * to * to last 21 sts. Yo, k2 tog, k2, ssk, yo, p1, k1, p1, yo, k2 tog, k2, ssk, yo, k6.

Row 38. K1, ssk, yo, ssk, k1, p6, k1, p1, k1, p6. * k6, yo, k2 tog, k2, ssk, yo, p3, k1, p2, yo, k2 tog, k2, ssk, yo, k1, ssk, yo, ssk, k1, p6, k1, p1, k1, p6 *. Repeat from * to * to last 6 sts. K6.

Row 39. K1, ssk, yo, ssk, k1, * yo, k2 tog, k2, ssk, yo, p1, k1, p1, yo, k2 tog, k2, ssk, yo, k5, p6, k2, p1, k3, p6, k1, ssk, yo, ssk, k1 *. Repeat from * to * to last 20 sts. Yo, k2 tog, k2, ssk, yo, p1, k1, p1, yo, k2 tog, k2, ssk, yo, k5.

Row 40. K1, ssk, yo, k2, p6, k1, m1, p1, m1, k1, p6, * k5, yo, k2 tog, k2, ssk, yo, p3, k1, p2, yo, k2 tog, k2, ssk, yo, k2, yo, k1, yo, k2, p6, k1, m1, p1, m1, k1, p6 *. Repeat from * to * to last 5 sts. K5.

Row 41. K1, ssk, yo, k2, * yo, k2 tog, k2, ssk, yo, p2, k1, p2, yo, k2 tog, k2, ssk, yo, k7, p6, ssk, p1, sl 2, k1, p2sso, p6, k2, yo, k1, yo, k2 *. Repeat from * to * to last 22 sts. Yo, k2 tog, k2, ssk, yo, p2, k1, p2, yo, k2 tog, k2, ssk, yo, k5.

Row 42. K1, ssk, yo, k2, p6, k2, p1, k2, p6, * k7, yo, k2 tog, k2, ssk, yo, sl 2, k1, p2sso, yo, k2 tog, k2, ssk, yo, k2, yo, k1, yo, k2 tog, yo, k2, p6, k2, p1, k2, p6 *. Repeat from * to * to last 5 sts. K5.

Row 43. K1, ssk, yo, k2, * yo, k2 tog, k2, ssk, yo, p2, k1, p2, yo, k2 tog, k2, ssk, yo, k9, p6, p2 tog, p5, k2, yo, k1, yo, k2 tog, yo, k2 *. Repeat from * to * to last 22 sts. Yo, k2 tog, k2, ssk, yo, p2, k1, p2, yo, k2 tog, k2, ssk, yo, k5.

Row 44. K1, ssk, yo, k2, p6, k2, p1, k2, p6, * k9, yo, k2 tog, k8, ssk, yo, k1, (k2 tog, yo,)three times, k2, p6, k2, p1, k2, p6 *. Repeat from * to * to last 5 sts. K5.

Row 45. K1, ssk, yo, k2, * yo, k2 tog, k2, ssk, yo, p2, k1, p2, yo, k2 tog, k2, ssk, yo, k9, p12, k1, (k2 tog, yo,) three times k2 *. Repeat from * to * to last 22 sts. Yo, k2 tog, k2, ssk, yo, p2, k1, p2, yo, k2 tog, k2, ssk, yo, k5.

Row 46. K1, ssk, yo, k2, p6, k2, m1, p1, k2, p6, * k9, yo, k2 tog, k8, ssk, yo, k2, (k2 tog, yo,)twice, k2 tog, k1, p6, k2, m1, p1, k2, p6 *. Repeat from * to * to last 5 sts. K5.

Row 47. K1, ssk, yo, k2, * yo, k2 tog, k2, ssk, yo, p2, k1, p3, yo, k2 tog, k2, ssk, yo, k8, p12, k2, (k2 tog, yo,)twice, k2 tog, k1 *. Repeat from * to * to last 23 sts. Yo, k2 tog, k2, ssk, yo, p2, k1, p3, yo, k2 tog, k2, ssk, yo, k5.

Row 48. K1, ssk, yo, k2, p6, k3, p1, k2, p6, * k8, yo, k2 tog, k8, ssk, yo, k1, (k2 tog, yo,)twice, k2 tog, k1, p6, k3, p1, k2, p6 *. Repeat from * to * to last 5 sts. K5.

Row 49. K1, ssk, yo, k2, * yo, k2 tog, k2, ssk, yo, p2, k1, p3, yo, k2 tog, k2, ssk, yo, k7, p12, k1, (k2 tog, yo,)twice, k2 tog, k1 *. Repeat from * to * to last 23 sts. Yo, k2 tog, k2, ssk, yo, p2, k1, p3, yo, k2 tog, k2, ssk, yo, k5.

Row 50. K1, ssk, yo, k2, p6, k3, p1, k2, p6, * k7, yo, k2 tog, k2, ssk, yo, m3, yo, k2 tog, k2, ssk, yo, k2, k2 tog, yo, k2 tog, k1, p6, k3, p1, k2, p6 *. Repeat from * to * to last 5 sts. K5.

Row 51. K1, ssk, yo, k2, * yo, k2 tog, k2, ssk, yo, p2, k1, p3, yo, k2 tog, k2, ssk, yo, k6, p6, k1, p1, k1, p6, k2, ssk, yo, ssk, k1 *. Repeat from * to * to last 23 sts. Yo, k2 tog, k2, ssk, yo, p2, k1, p3, yo, k2 tog, k2, ssk, yo, k5.

Row 52. K1, ssk, yo, k2, p6, k3, p1, k2, p6, * k6, yo, k2 tog, k2, ssk, yo, p1, k1, p1, yo, k2 tog, k2, ssk, yo, k1, k2 tog, yo, k2 tog, k1, p6, k3, p1, k2, p6 *. Repeat from * to * to last 5 sts. K5.

Row 53. K1, ssk, yo, k2, * yo, k2 tog, k2, ssk, yo, p2, k1, p3, yo, k2 tog, k2, ssk, yo, k5, p6, k1, p1, k1, p6, k1, k2 tog, yo, k2 tog, k1 *. Repeat from * to * to last 23 sts. Yo, k2 tog, k2, ssk, yo, p2, k1, p3, yo, k2 tog, k2, ssk, yo, k5.

Row 54. K1, ssk, yo, k2, p6, k3, p1, k2, p6, * k5, yo, k2 tog, k2, ssk, yo, p1, k1, p1, yo, k2 tog, k2, ssk, yo, k1, k2 tog, yo, k2, p6, k3, p1, k2, p6 *. Repeat from * to * to last 5 sts. K5.

Row 55. K2, yo, k1, yo, k2, * yo, k2 tog, k2, ssk, yo, p2, k1, p3, yo, k2 tog, k2, ssk, yo, k5, p6, k1, m1, p1, m1, k1, p6, k2, yo, k1, yo, k2 *. Repeat from * to * to last 23 sts. Yo, k2 tog, k2, ssk, yo, p2, k1, p3, yo, k2 tog, k2, ssk, yo, k5.

Row 56. K2, yo, k1, yo, k2, p6, sl 2, k1, p2sso, p1, k2 tog, p6, * k7, yo, k2 tog, k2, ssk, yo, p2, k1, p2, yo, k2 tog, k2, ssk, yo, k2, yo, k1, yo, k2, p6, sl 2, k1, p2sso, p1, k2 tog, p6 *. Repeat from * to * to last 7 sts. K7.

Row 57. K2, yo, ssk, yo, k1, yo, k2, * yo, k2 tog, k2, ssk, yo, sl 2, k1, p2sso, yo, k2 tog, k2, ssk, yo, k7, p6, k2, p1, k2, p6, k2, yo, ssk, yo, k1, yo, k2 *. Repeat from * to * to last 22 sts. Yo, k2 tog, k2, ssk, yo, sl 2, k1, p2sso, yo, k2 tog, k2, ssk, yo, k7.

Row 58. K2, yo, ssk, yo, k1, yo, k2, p5, p2 tog, p6, * k9, yo, k2 tog, k2, ssk, yo, p2, k1, p2, yo, k2 tog, k2, ssk, yo, k2, yo, ssk, yo, k1, yo, k2, p5, p2 tog, p6 *. Repeat from * to * to last 9 sts. K9.

Row 59. K2, (yo, k2 tog,) three times, k1, * yo, k2 tog, k8, ssk, yo, k9, p6, k2, p1, k2, p6, k2, (yo, ssk,) three times, k1 *. Repeat from * to * to last 21 sts. Yo, k2 tog, k8, ssk, yo, k9.

Row 60. K2, (yo, ssk,) three times, k1, p12, * k9, yo, k2 tog, k2, ssk, yo, p2, k1, p2, yo, k2 tog, k2, ssk, yo, k2, (yo, ssk,) three times, k1, p12 *. Repeat from * to * to last 9 sts. K9.

Cast on 311 stitches loosely. Knit ten rows in garter stitch increasing in the first and last stitch of rows 1,3,5,7, and 9. (321 stitches.)

Begin working the 60 rows of the pattern either from the written instructions or the chart. Figure 177. At the same time, continue to increase one stitch at each end of each alternate row five more times and knit these extra stitches in garter stitch. (331 stitches).

The 60 pattern rows are worked seven times to complete the centre, keeping the five extra stitches at each end as a border of garter stitch until row 50 of the seventh pattern. For the last ten rows decrease one stitch at each end of each alternate row (321 stitches). Work nine rows in garter stitch, continuing to decrease at each end of each alternate row. (311 stitches).

Work the tenth row as follows:

K5, k2 tog,* k2, k2 tog *. Repeat from * to * to last 5 sts. K5. (210 stitches). Do not break yarn.

The border is knitted on to these stitches. For the corners pick up 15 stitches along the diagonal created by the increases/ decreases and for each side pick up one stitch for every two rows. (210 stitches). The cast-on edge loops are picked up by beginning with one stitch for each of the first five loops and then two of every three loops until the last five loops when each loop is used. (210 stitches).

I do not pick up all the stitches at once, but in sections as required.

The size of the shawl can be varied by working within multiples of 30 rows or 15 stitches on which to work the edging.

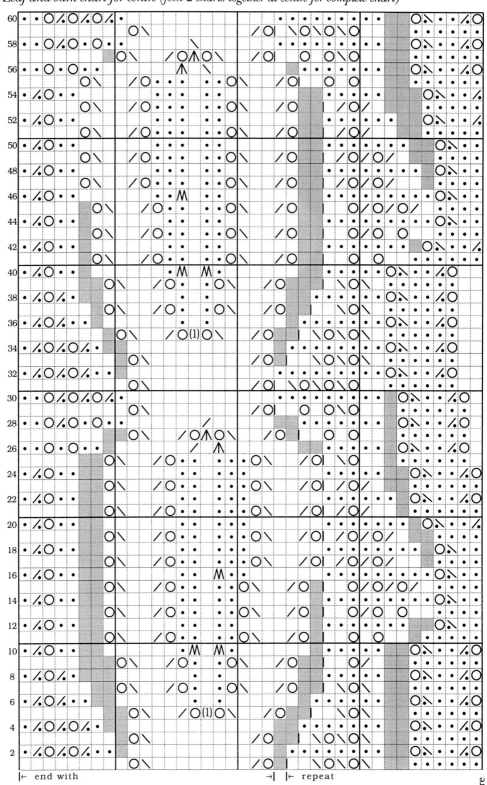

Figure 177. Leaf and bark chart for centre (join 2 charts together at centre for complete chart)

centre

Key to numerals for both charts
(1) = m3 ie work k1, p1, k1 through back of lifted thread between stitches.
(2) = sl st wyif after knitting once into 3 loops below.
(3) = IncB w2 tog ie with yarn at back sl2 then bring yarn forward, replace both
slipped stitches back onto left-hand needle and IncB in both sts together.

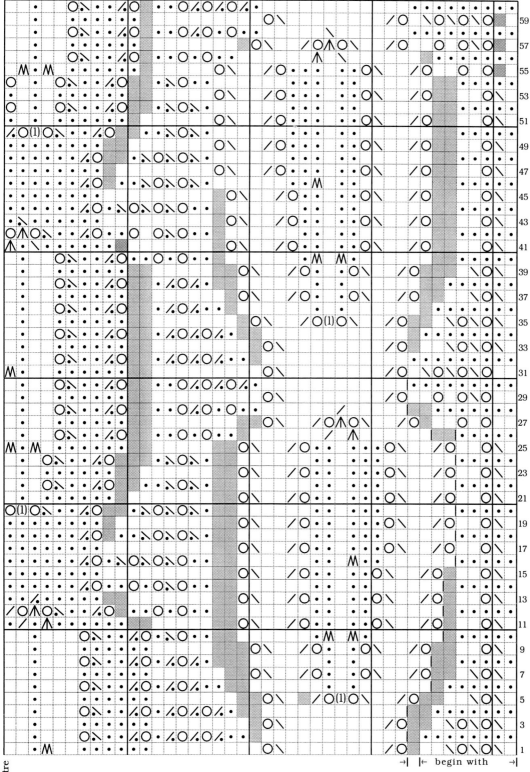

Pattern for edging

Chart shown in Figure 178.

Take a length of crochet cotton and make a loose chain of 12 loops as a foundation for the first row of the pattern which is worked into these loops which are placed on to the left-hand needle, with the centre of the shawl on the right-hand needle.

Row 1. K2, k2 tog, yo, (k2 tog) twice, (yo, k2 tog) twice.

Row 2. Cast on loosely 17 sts, k25, yo, sl 2, k1 (from shawl sts), p2sso, turn. NB On all even rows the last stitch is knitted from the shawl to attach the border.

Row 3. K2, (k2 tog, yo) three times, k2, k2 tog, (yo, k1) nine times, k2 tog, yo, m3, (yo, ssk) twice.

Row 4. K4, p1, k1, p1, k29, yo, sl 2, k1, p2sso turn.

Row 5. K3, (k2 tog, yo) twice, k3, k2 tog, yo, (K1 elongated twice, ie knit one stitch wrapping yarn three times around needle. Drop extra wraps from needle in following row) 15 times, yo, ssk, k2 tog, yo, k1, p1, k1, (yo, ssk) twice.

Row 6. K4, p1, k1, p1, k4, (slip next 3 sts dropping extra wraps, return to left hand needle, k3 tog) five times, k10, yo, sl 2, k1, p2sso. Turn.

Row 7. K2, (k2 tog, yo) three times, m3, yo, ssk, k2 tog, yo, (slip next stitch with yarn forward but before doing so knit one stitch through 3 loops of row below) five times, yo, ssk, k2 tog, yo, k1, p1, k1, (yo, ssk) twice.

Row 8. K4, p1, m1 purlwise, k1, m1 purlwise, p1, k4, (k1, sl 1 wyif) five times, k4, (incB) three times, k6, yo, sl 2, k1, p2sso. Turn.

Row 9. K3, k2 tog, yo, k1, k2 tog, yo, incB, k4, incB, yo, ssk, k2 tog, yo, (k1, sl 1 wyif) five times, yo, ssk, k2 tog, yo, k2, p1, k2, (yo, ssk) twice.

Row 10. K4, p2, k1, p2, k4, (k1, sl 1 wyif) five times, k4, (incB, k6) twice, yo, sl 2, k1, p2sso. Turn.

Row 11. K2, k2 tog, yo, k2, k2 tog, yo, incB, k2, k2 tog, yo, ssk, k2, incB, yo, ssk, k2 tog, yo, ssk, (k1, sl 1 wyif) three times, ssk, yo, ssk, k2 tog, yo, k2, p1, k2, (yo, ssk) twice.

Row 12. K4, p2, k1, p2, k4, k2 tog, (sl 1 wyif, k1) twice, p2 tog, k9, knit into front and back of yo loop, k11, yo, sl 2, k1, p2sso. Turn.

Row 13. K4, (k2 tog) twice, yo, k2, k2 tog, yo, ssk, k2 tog, yo, ssk, k2, yo, ssk, k2 tog, yo, ssk, k1, sl 1 wyif, ssk, yo, ssk, k2 tog, yo, k2, p1, k2, (yo, ssk) twice.

Figure 178. Flower and leaf border.

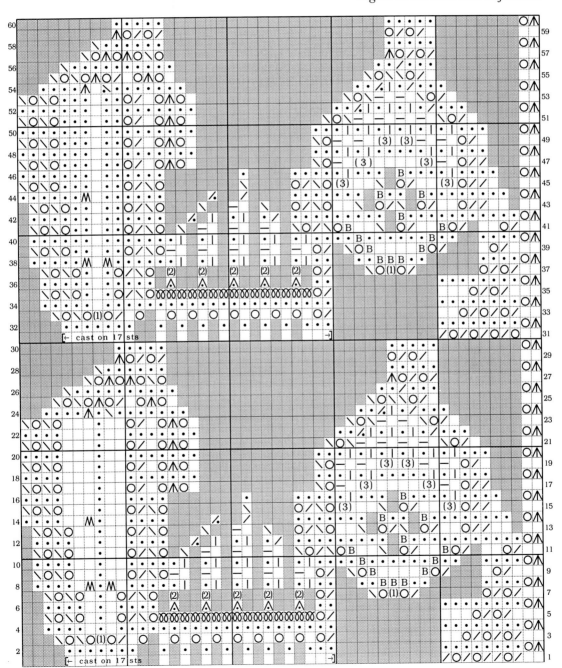

Row 14. K4, p2, m1, k1, p2, k4, k2 tog, p2 tog, k7, incB, k2, incB, k8, yo, sl 2, k1, p2sso. Turn.

Row 15. K3, (k2 tog)twice, yo, incB w2 tog as follows: with yarn at back sl 2 then bring yarn forward replace both slipped stitches back onto left-hand needle and incB in both sts together, k2, k2 tog, yo, ssk, k2, incB w2 tog, yo, ssk, k2 tog, yo, ssk, yo, ssk, k2 tog, yo, k2, p1, k3, (yo, ssk)twice.

Row 16. K4, p3, k1, p2, k10, sl 1 wyif, k3, incB, k4, sl 1 wyif, k4, yo, sl 2, k1, p2sso. Turn.

Row 17. K2, (k2 tog)twice, yo, k1, sl 1 wyif, incB w2 tog, k4, incB w2 tog, k1, sl 1 wyif, yo, ssk, k1, yo, sl 2, k1, p2sso, yo, k1, k2 tog, yo, k2, p1, k3, (yo, ssk)twice.

Row 18. K4, p3, k1, p2, k10, (sl 1 wyif, k1)twice, k4, (sl 1 wyif, k1)twice, k2, yo, sl 2, k1, p2sso. Turn.

Row 19. K3, k2 tog, yo, (k1, sl 1 wyif)twice, (incB w2 tog)twice, (k1, sl 1 wyif)twice, yo, ssk, k1, yo, sl 2, k1, p2sso, yo, k1, k2 tog, yo, k2, p1, k3, (yo, ssk)twice.

Row 20. K4, p3, k1, p2, k10, (sl 1 wyif, k1)six times, k2, yo, sl 2, k1, p2sso. Turn.

Row 21. K3, k2 tog, yo, ssk, (k1, sl 1 wyif)four times, ssk, yo, ssk, k1, yo, sl 2, k1, p2sso, yo, k1, k2 tog, yo, k2, p1, k3, (yo, ssk)twice.

Row 22. K4, p3, k1, p2, k9, k2 tog, (sl 1 wyif, k1)three times, p2 tog, k3, yo, sl 2, k1, p2sso. Turn.

Row 23. K3, k2 tog, yo, ssk, (k1, sl 1 wyif)twice, ssk, yo, ssk, k1, yo, sl 2, k1, p2sso, k1, k2 tog, yo, k2, p1, k3, (yo, ssk) twice.

Row 24. K4, p3 tog, k1, p2 tog, k9, k2 tog, sl 1 wyif, k1, p2 tog, k3, yo, sl 2, k1, p2sso. Turn.

Row 25. K3, k2 tog, yo, (ssk)twice, yo, ssk, k1, yo, sl 2, k1, p2sso, yo, k1, k2 tog, yo, sl 2, k1, p2sso, (yo, ssk)twice.

Row 26. K2 tog, k12, p2 tog, k3, yo, sl 2, k1, p2sso. Turn.

Row 27. K2, (k2 tog, yo)twice, sl 2, k1, p2sso, yo, k2 tog, (yo, sl 2, k1, p2sso)twice, yo, ssk.

Row 28. K2 tog, k11, yo, sl 2, k1, p2sso. Turn.

Row 29. K3, (k2 tog, yo)four times, sl 2, k1, p2sso.

Row 30. K10, yo, sl 2, k1, p2sso. Turn.

Rows 31, 32 and **33** as rows 1, 2, and 3.

Row 34. K5, p1, k30, yo, sl 2, k1, p2sso. Turn.

Row 35. K3, (k2 tog, yo)twice, k3, k2 tog, yo, (k1 elongated twice)fifteen times, yo, ssk, k2 tog, yo, p1, k1, p1, (yo, ssk)twice.

Row 36. K5, p1, k5, (k3long tog)five times, k10, yo, sl 2, k1, p2sso. Turn.

Row 37. K2, (k2 tog, yo)three times, m3, yo, ssk, k2 tog, yo, (slip st wyif after knitting once into 3 loops below)five times, yo, ssk, k2 tog, yo, p1, k1, p1, (yo, ssk) twice.

Row 38. K5, m1, p1, m1, k6, (sl 1 wyif, k1) five times, k3, (incB) three times, k6, yo, sl 2, k1, p2sso. Turn.

Row 39. K3, k2 tog, yo, k1, k2 tog, yo, incB, k4, incB, yo, ssk, k2 tog, yo, (k1, sl 1 wyif) five times, yo, ssk, k2 tog, yo, p2, k1, p2, (yo, ssk) twice.

Row 40. K6, p1, k7, (sl 1 wyif, k1) five times, k3, (incB, k6) twice, yo, sl 2, k1, p2sso. Turn.

Row 41. K2, k2 tog, yo, k2, k2 tog, yo, incB, k2, k2 tog, yo, ssk, k2, incB, yo, ssk, k2 tog, yo, ssk, (k1, sl 1 wyif) three times, ssk, yo, ssk, k2 tog, yo, p2, k1, p2, (yo, ssk) twice.

Row 42. K6, p1, k6, k2 tog, (sl 1 wyif, k1) twice, p2 tog, K9, incB, k11, yo, sl 2, k1, p2sso. Turn.

Row 43. K4, (k2 tog) twice, yo, k2, k2 tog, yo, ssk, k2 tog, yo, ssk, k2, yo, ssk, k2 tog, yo, ssk, k1, sl 1 wyif, ssk, yo, ssk, k2 tog, yo, p2, k1, p2, (yo, ssk) twice.

Row 44. K6, m1, p1, k6, k2 tog, p2 tog, k7, incB, k2, incB, k8, yo, sl 2, k1, p2sso. Turn.

Row 45. K3, (k2 tog) twice, yo, incB w2 tog, k2, k2 tog, yo, ssk, k2, incB w2 tog, yo, ssk, k2 tog, (yo, ssk) twice, k2 tog, yo, p2, k1, p3, (yo, ssk) twice.

Row 46. K7, p1, k12, sl 1 wyif, k3, incB, k4, sl 1 wyif, k4, yo, sl 2, k1, p2sso. Turn.

Row 47. K2, (k2 tog) twice, yo, k1, sl 1 wyif, incB w2 tog, k4, incB w2 tog, k1, sl 1 wyif, yo, ssk, k1, yo, sl 2, k1, p2sso, yo, k1, k2 tog, yo, p2, k1, p3, (yo, ssk) twice.

Row 48. K7, p1, k12, (sl 1 wyif, k1) twice, k4, (sl 1 wyif, k1) twice, k2, yo, sl 2, k1, p2sso. Turn.

Row 49. K3, k2 tog, yo, (k1, sl 1 wyif) twice, (incB w2 tog) twice, (k1, sl 1 wyif) twice, yo, ssk, k1, yo, sl 2, k1, p2sso, yo, k1, k2 tog, yo, p2, k1, p3, (yo, ssk) twice.

Row 50. K7, p1, k12, (sl 1 wyif, k1) six times, k2, yo, sl 2, k1, p2sso. Turn.

Row 51. K3, k2 tog, yo, ssk, (k1, sl 1 wyif) four times, ssk, yo, ssk, k1, yo, sl 2, k1, p2sso, yo, k1, k2 tog, yo, p2, k1, p3, (yo, ssk) twice.

Row 52. K7, p1, k11, k2 tog, (sl 1 wyif, k1) three times, p2 tog, k3, yo, sl 2, k1, p2sso. Turn.

Row 53. K3, k2 tog, yo, ssk, (k1, sl 1 wyif) twice, ssk, yo, ssk, k1, yo, sl 2, k1, p2sso, yo, k1, k2 tog, yo, p2, k1, p3, (yo, ssk) twice.

Row 54. K4, sl 2, k1, p2sso, k1, k2 tog, k9, k2 tog, sl 1 wyif, k1, p2 tog, k3, yo, sl 2, k1, p2sso. Turn.

Rows 55 to **60** as rows 25 to 30.

When all the stitches picked up from the four sides of the centre of the shawl have been worked off with the border, graft the remaining border stitches to the stitches of the first row of the border. To do this place a knitting needle through these stitches to hold them before unravelling the crochet cotton.

Finally wash and block the shawl according to the instructions in Appendix A, with sufficient tension to open up the pattern, but not so much as to lose the texture created by the stocking stitch and reverse stocking stitch areas.

Appendix F

૨**ૡ**

Bibliography

Books

Abbey, Barbara. *Barbara Abbey's Knitting Lace.* First published 1974 The Viking Press Inc. 1993 edition, The Schoolhouse Press, Wisconsin.

Anderson, Lee. *You Knit Unique.* New Zealand Wool Board, Wellington, New Zealand 1985.

Bennett, Helen M. *Scottish Knitting.* (Shire Album 164) 1986.

Burda 400 Knitpatterns E519. Printed and published by Verlag Aenne Burda, Am Kestendemm 2, D-7600 Offenburg, West Germany.

_____ . *Lace Knitting, E294 1994.*

Carter, Hazel. *Shetland Lace Knitting from Charts.* Hazel Carter, Madison, Wisconsin 1988.

Don, Sarah. *The Art of Shetland Lace.* First published Mills and Boon Ltd, London 1980. Lacis, Berkeley Calif 1991.

Edwards, Betty. *Drawing on the Right Side of the Brain.* Fontana, London 1979.

Hiatt, June Hemmons. *The Principles of Knitting.* Simon and Schuster, New York 1988.

Kinzel, Marianne. *First Book of Modern Lace Knitting.* First published Mills and Boon Ltd, London 1953. Dover Publications Inc., New York 1972.

_____ . *Second Book of Modern Lace Knitting.* First published Mills and Boon Ltd, London 1961. Dover Publications Inc., New York 1972.

Kliot, Jules & Kaethe. *The Knitted Lace Patterns of Christine Duchrow, V-1.* Lacis, Berkeley Calif 1993.

_____ . *The Knitted Lace Patterns of Christine Duchrow, V-2.* Lacis, Berkeley Calif 1994.

Lewis, Susanna E. *Knitting Lace.* Taunton Press, Newtown CT, 1992.

Lorant, Tessa. *The Batsford Book of Hand and Machine Knitted Laces.* B.T. Batsford Ltd., London 1982.

Messent, Jan. *Wool 'n Magic.* Search Press, Kent, United Kingdom 1989.

Mon Tricot. *The Knitting Dictionary* (translation Margaret Hamilton-Hunt). Crown Publishers, New York 1971.

_____ . *The Key to Success. Step by Step Knitting.* Ste. Ediclair et Cie, Paris 1981.

Niedner, Marie & von Reden, Gussi. *Knitted Lace (Kunst-Stricken).* First published by Verlag Otto Beyer, Leipzig, 1920. Lacis Berkeley.

Nicolaides, Kimon. *The Natural way to Draw.* Houghton Mifflin Co., Boston 1941.

Norbury, James. *Traditional Knitting Patterns.* First published B.T. Batsford Ltd, London 1962. Dover Publications Inc., New York 1973.

Penning, Gloria (compiled by). *Patterns for the Art of Lace Knitting, The Complete Works of Rachel Schnelling.* Heirloom Lace, Missouri 1991.

Phillips, Mary Walker. *Creative Knitting: A New Art Form.* Van Nostrand Reinhold Company, New York 1980.

Reade, Dorothy. *25 Original Knitting Designs.* Dorothy Reade, Eugene, Oregan 1968.

Rutt, Richard. *A History of Knitting.* B.T. Batsford Ltd, London 1987, Interweave Press, Colorado 1987.

Thomas, Mary. *Mary Thomas's Knitting Book.* First published Hodder and Stoughton, Ltd., London, 1938. 1972 edition, Dover Publications Inc., New York.

_____ . *Mary Thomas's Book of Knitting Patterns.* First published Hodder and Stoughton Ltd., London, 1943. 1972 edition, Dover Publications Inc., New York.

Walker, Barbara G. *A Treasury of Knitting Patterns.* Charles Scribner's Sons, New York 1968.

_____ . *A Second Treasury of Knitting Patterns.* Charles Scribner's Sons, New York 1970.

_____ . *The Craft of Lace Knitting.* Charles Scribner's Sons, New York 1971.

_____ . *Charted Knitting Designs.* Charles Scribner's Sons, New York 1972.

Zimmerman, Elizabeth. *Knitting Without Tears.* Charles Scribner's Sons, New York 1971.

Services

Russell, Janet. *Lace Index.* Janet Russell, 5423 S. Dorchester Ave., Chicago, IL 60615.

Stanley, Montse. *Knitting Reference Library.* Montse Stanley, P.O. Box 471, Cambridge, CB5 8XF. England.

Jamieson & Smith Ltd. *Brochure of Shetland knitting patterns and yarn packs.* Jamieson & Smith Ltd., 90 North Road, Lerwick ZE1 0PQ. United Kingdom.

Index

❧

Creating Original Hand-Knitted Lace

Appendices not included